ANTIQUARIES
OF
GLOUCESTERSHIRE
AND BRISTOL

Uxori, comiti, adiutrici meae
per xlv annos
M.M.G.

ANTIQUARIES OF GLOUCESTERSHIRE AND BRISTOL

By
Irvine Gray

BRISTOL AND GLOUCESTERSHIRE
ARCHAEOLOGICAL SOCIETY
1981

Bristol and Gloucestershire
Archaeological Society
9 Pembroke Road
Clifton
Bristol   BS8 3AU

© Irvine Gray, 1981

ISBN 0 900197 14 5

Produced for the Society by
Alan Sutton Publishing Limited, Gloucester.
Printed in Great Britain by
Redwood Burn Limited, Trowbridge and Esher.

Apologia

... if any of you shall observe any slip of pen, number, marginall, or other small mistake (which, I hope, at the most are few, if any) that yee would reforme them favourably, and fairly say ...... that men and the works of men are not born perfect and with beards upon their chins .....; figures or notes in my pocket-paper-books cursorily taken in my searches may bee mistaken, or my clarks erre in often transcribing .....
John Smith, Lives of the Berkeleys, (1618), II, 444.

Peruse with heed, then freendly judge,
and blaming rash refraine:
So maist thou reade to thy delight
and eke requit my paine.

William Adams, Chronicle (1625)

It may be observed, perhaps, as a peculiarity in some part of these Memoirs, that much of it consists of quotations. I have not done this without due consideration, ... the words of the original writer carry you back into the manners and language and sentiments and party-spirit of the age in which he wrote .... By these means local history assumes a national character, and pursuits of the Antiquary are blended with those of the Historian, from which they should never have been separated.
Samuel Seyer, Memoirs etc. of Bristol (1821-25), preface.

We antiquaries are considered by very many as imbecils, or at best old women.
Thomas Dudley Fosbroke, in a letter to John Nichols,
his publisher.

Contents

List of Illustrations 9
Abbreviations 13
Preface and Acknowledgements 15
Introduction 17

The Antiquaries:
1. William WORCESTRE alias BOTONER, 1415 - c. 1485
2. Robert RICART, fl. 1466 - 1508
3. John SMITH ('Smith of Nibley'), 1567 - 1641
4. William ADAMS, c. 1585 - c. 1650
5. John THEYER, ?1598 - 1673
6. Abel WANTNER, ?1639 - 1714
7. Richard PARSONS, 1643 - 1711
8. Sir Robert ATKYNS, 1647 - 1711
9. John PRINN or PRYNNE, 1661 or 1662 - 1735
10. Richard GRAVES, 1677 - 1729
11. Richard FURNEY, 1694 - 1753
12. George BALLARD, 1706 - 1755
13. Ralph BIGLAND, 1711 - 1784
14. Samuel RUDDER, 1726 - 1801
15. William BARRETT, ?1727 - 1789
16. Thomas RUDGE, 1753 - 1825
17. Samuel SEYER, 1757 - 1831
18. George Worrall COUNSEL, 1758 - 1843
19. Daniel LYSONS, 1762 - 1834
20. Samuel LYSONS, 1763 - 1819
21. James DALLAWAY, 1763 - 1834
22. John Delafield PHELPS, 1764 or 5 - 1842
23. Thomas Dudley FOSBROKE, 1770 - 1842
24. George Weare BRAIKENRIDGE, 1775 - 1856
25. Paul Hawkins FISHER, 1779 - 1873
26. John EVANS, 1784 - 1831
27. George ORMEROD, 1785 - 1873
28. James BENNETT, 1785 - 1856
29. William TYSON, 1785 - 1851
30. Henry Thomas ELLACOMBE, 1790 - 1885

31. Samuel Roffey MAITLAND, 1792 - 1866
32. Sir Thomas PHILLIPPS, Bt., 1792 - 1872
33. John Daniel Thomas NIBLETT, 1809 - 1883
34. Sir John MACLEAN, 1811 - 1895
35. Thomas KERSLAKE, 1812 - 1891
36. John GODING, 1816 - 1879
37. David ROYCE, 1817 - 1902
38. Beaver Henry BLACKER, 1821 - 1890
39. Henry George NICHOLLS, 1822 - 1867
40. John LATIMER, 1824 - 1904
41. John Randall CLARKE, 1827 or 1828 - 1863
42. John TAYLOR, 1829 - 1893
43. William GEORGE, 1830 - 1900
44. Francis Frederick FOX, 1833 - 1915
45. William BAZELEY, 1843 - 1925
46. Sir Francis Adams HYETT, 1844 - 1941
47. Charles Samuel TAYLOR, 1848 - 1925
48. William Phillimore Watts PHILLIMORE, 1853 - 1913
49. Frank Step HOCKADAY, 1855 - 1924
50. Welbore St. Clair BADDELEY, 1856 - 1946
51. William Henry KNOWLES, 1857 - 1943
52. Roland AUSTIN, 1874 - 1954

Illustrations of Handwriting 140-199
Index 201

Illustrations of Handwriting
(in chronological order, numbered as for the Antiquaries)

The illustrations are reproduced by kind permission of:- No. 1a, The Master and Fellows of Corpus Christi College, Cambridge; Nos. 1b, 8, 9, 11, 13, 14, 16, 19, 23, 25, 30, 46 and 48, the Gloucestershire Record Office; Nos. 2, 4, 15, 17, 44, and 47, the Bristol Record Office; Nos. 3, 22, 26, 31, 33, 38, 45, 49 and 50, the Gloucester Library; Nos. 5, 6, 7, 10, 12, 18 and 32, The Bodleian Library, Oxford; No. 20, The Society of Antiquaries of London; Nos. 21, 24, 29, 35, 40, 42, Bristol Central Library; No. 27, P.J. Ormerod, esq.; Nos. 28 and 51, The British Library; No. 34, The Royal Institution of Cornwall; No. 36, the Committee of Bayshill Unitarian Church, Cheltenham; No. 37, the Bristol and Gloucestershire Archaeological Society; No. 39, the Public Record Office; No. 41, the Fitzwilliam Museum, Cambridge; No. 43, Messrs. William George's Sons, Ltd, Bristol; No. 52, Gerard Leighton, esq.

1a	William Worcestre	A note on Cirencester, etc., 1480 (Worcestre's Itineraries, Corpus Christi, Cambridge MS. 210, f. 205)
1b.	William Worcestre	Letter to the churchwardens of Oxenton, Glos. 1456 (G.R.O., D1637 M.13)
2.	Robert Ricart	Bristol and national history, 1484-85 (The Maire's Kalendar, B.R.O. 04720)
3.	John Smith of Nibley	'Rules for the kepinge my clocke' (Glos. Coll. 13605, vol.5)
4.	William Adams	The Bristol v. Exeter shooting-match, etc., 1616-17 (Adams's Chronicle, B.R.O. 13748(4))
5.	John Theyer	Letter to Anthony Wood, 2 Feb. 1662/3 Bodl. MS. Wood, D 45, f. 22)
6.	Abel Wantner	Letter, n.d., seeking genealogical information (Bodl. MS. Top. Gloucs., c.2 (S.C. 27827), 190)
7.	Richard Parsons	(Part) description of N. Cerney, from his 'Parochial Visitation' (Bodl. MS. Rawl., B 323, f. 56)

8. Sir Robert Atkyns, jun. Signature on deed, 1702 (G.R.O., D2113/2)
9. John Prinn or Prynne From memoranda in Cheltenham manor court book (G.R.O., D 855 M 12)
10. Richard Graves (Part) letter to Thomas Hearne, 1723 (Bodl. Rawl. lett.6 (S.C. 15572), 140a)
11. Richard Furney 'As sure as God is at Gloucester' (G.R.O. D.327)
12. George Ballard Letter (abbreviated) to Thomas Hearne, 1732 (Bodl. Rawl. lett.6 (S.C. 15572), 2/249)
13. Ralph Bigland From a letter to the Rev. H.G. Dobyns-Yate, 1780 (G.R.O., Pc 179)
14. Samuel Rudder From a draft description of Lydney, sent to Charles Bragge Bathurst, n.d. (G.R.O. D421 E 27)
15. William Barrett From a letter to George Catcott, 1788 (B.R.O. 15266)
16. Thomas Rudge From the parish register of St. Michael's, Gloucester, 1784 (G.R.O., P 154/14 IN 1/3)
17. Samuel Seyer (Part of) draft letter to the Bishop of Bristol, 1822 (B.R.O. 12147(52))
18. G.W. Counsel Letter to Sir Thomas Phillipps, about a sale of Furney MSS., 1834 (Bodl. MS. Phillipps Robinson, c.451, fol. 108)
19. Daniel Lysons (Part of) draft letter to Charles Bragge Bathurst, n.d., concerning Samuel Lysons's books (G.R.O., D. 853/4)
20. Samuel Lysons Drawing of font from St. Mary de Crypt, Gloucester, n.d. (Soc. of Antiquaries MS. 782/7)
21. James Dallaway (Part of) letter to G.W. Braikenridge, 1828. (Bris. L. 23999)
22. J.D. Phelps Note on fly-leaf of book (Gloucester Library, Clifford Coll.)
23. T.D. Fosbroke Letter to Nathaniel Clifford, 1802 (G.R.O. D 149 F 42)
24. G.W. Braikenridge (Part of) letter to John Britton, F.S.A., 1830 (Bris. L. 22992)
25. P.H. Fisher Notes on Stroud church, n.d. (G.R.O., D1842 H 2)

26. John Evans — Note inserted in copy of Tyson's *Bristol Memorialist* (Glos. Coll. 5353)
27. George Ormerod — Note on records of Beachley and Chepstow area (From volume in possession of Mr. P.J. Ormerod, 1979)
28. James Bennett — Note, presenting book to Nichols & Son, publishers (In British Library copy of his *Tewkesbury Register*)
29. William Tyson — Queries about Bristol inns (Bris. L. Jefferies Coll.)
30. H.T. Ellacombe — Letter on bell-ringing customs, 1875 (G.R.O., P217 CW 4/13)
31. S.R. Maitland — The quarrel between Bishop Miles Smith and Dean Laud (Glos. Coll. 2091)
32. Sir Thomas Phillipps, Bt. — Draft reply to G.W. Counsel (See Ill. No. 18)(Bodl., MS. Phillipps-Robinson, c.451, fol.108)
33. J.D.T. Niblett — Notes on stained glass in Fairford church (Glos. Coll. 8267)
34. Sir John Maclean — (Part of) letter to the Rev. W. Jago, on the Society of Antiquaries, etc., 1871 (Brooks Coll., R. Institution of Cornwall)
35. Thomas Kerslake — (Part of) letter to the Council of the Bristol Museum and Library (Bris. L., B 26069)
36. John Goding — Page 1 of 'History of the Society' in the Transactions of the Cheltenham Unitarian Congregation, 1844
37. David Royce — (Part) abstract of Dutton pardon (1559) (B.G.A.S., Royce Papers 243, at Gloucester Library)
38. B.H. Blacker — From catalogue of his library (Glos. Coll. 12412, p. 114)
39. H.G. Nicholls — (Part of) letter to the Office of Works concerning Holy Trinity School, Drybrook, 1862 (P.R.O., F 3/209)
40. John Latimer — Note on the Rev. H.T. Ellacombe's MSS. (Bris. L., B 28264)
41. J.R. Clarke — (Part of) letter to J.G. Nichols on Roman finds in Gloucester, 1854 (Fitzwilliam Museum, Cambridge, MS. Perceval L 57)

42.	John Taylor	From his letter of resignation from the Bristol Museum and Library, 1883 (Bris. L., B 26069)
43.	William George	Recollections of his apprenticeship to William Strong, 1877 (from records of William George's Sons Ltd., Bristol)
44.	F.F. Fox	Note from MS. Calendar of deeds, 1878 (B.R.O. 08153/4)
45.	William Bazeley	From his notebooks (Glos. Coll. 6, vol. 1, p.139)
46.	Sir Francis Hyett	A priced list of books (G.R.O., D 6 F 133)
47.	C.S. Taylor	From a letter about early deeds of St. Thomas's, Bristol, 1924 (B.R.O., P/St. T. HM/17)
48.	W.P.W. Phillimore	Letter to the Vicar of Minsterworth, 1907 (Inserted in G.R.O. copy of Phillimore's Glos. Marr. Registers, Vol. 1)
49.	F.S. Hockaday	From his abstracts of Gloucester Consistory Court, 1551, for Frampton-on-Severn (Glos. Coll., Hockaday Abstracts)
50.	W. St. C. Baddeley	Romans and romance; from a notebook, 1908 (Glos. Coll. Baddeley 90, f. 45d)
51.	W.H. Knowles	Sketch of Saxon work in Jarrow church, Co. Durham, 1898 (B.L., Add. 37508, f.112)
52.	Roland Austin	From a letter to Wilfrid Leighton, 1 April 1943, on Bristol war damage and the Theatre Royal, Bristol (in the possession of Mr. Gerard Leighton, 1979)

Abbreviations

B.G.A.S.	Bristol & Gloucestershire Archaeological Society
Biog. Suppt.	The (Biographical) Supplement to the Bibliographer's Manual of Gloucestershire Literature (Hyett & Austin)
B.L.	British Library (formerly British Museum Library)
Bodl.	Bodleian Library, Oxford
B.R.O.	Bristol Record Office
Bris. L.	Bristol (Central) Library (Avon County Reference Library)
C.N.F.C.	Cotteswold Naturalists' Field Club
D.N.B.	Dictionary of National Biography
Gent.Mag.	The Gentleman's Magazine
Glos.Coll.	The Gloucestershire Collection, Gloucester Library
Glos. N. & Q.	Gloucestershire Notes & Queries
G.R.O.	Gloucestershire Record Office
Man. G. Lit.	(The Bibliographer's) Manual of Gloucestershire Literature (Hyett & Bazeley)
N. & Q.	Notes & Queries
N.R.A.	National Register of Archives (Hist. MSS. Commission)
P.R.O.	Public Record Office
TBGAS	Transactions of the Bristol & Gloucestershire Archaeological Society
V.C.H.	Victoria County History

Cross-references from one Antiquary to another are given by their serial numbers, in brackets; e.g. (No. 1).

Preface and Acknowledgements

This small book cannot claim originality. It was suggested by the useful and well-received *Topographers of Suffolk*, compiled by Dr. J.M. Blatchly, F.S.A., Headmaster of Ipswich School (*Alma Mater mea*) and published in 1976 by the Suffolk Record Office. It is intended to be a convenient guide book, and almost entirely factual. No serious criticism or assessment of our antiquaries has been undertaken, though the Introduction makes some attempt to show their relationship to one another.

Selection of the 'antiquaries' has not been altogether easy. None who died less than twenty-five years ago has been included. Roughly speaking, those whose field of research was confined to one rural parish, or to one limited subject, have been excluded, valuable though their work has sometimes been. Thus room could not be found for John Guillim (1565-1621), who came from Minsterworth, since he was purely a herald.[1] One would have liked to include the Quaker printer, John Bellows of Gloucester (1831-1902), but archaeology was only one of his many interests; or Ida Roper or Mary Rudd, who both did good work in the early part of the present century, but one seems to have written solely on church effigies, the other on the parish of Bisley. Indeed, some Quango concerned with sex discrimination may note disapprovingly that all the fifty-two chosen are men; but the fact is that until fairly recently antiquarian studies were almost exclusively a male pursuit; there were a few exceptions, but not, I think, in Gloucestershire or Bristol. However, a woman addressed our Archaeological Society as early as 1894, whereas a woman could not become a Fellow of the Society of Antiquaries until 1920.[2] Our women have more than made up for it since, with several distinguished Presidents of the Bristol and Gloucestershire Archaeological Society, and one of them, Dame Joan Evans, the first woman President of the Society of Antiquaries of London.

The arrangement is chronological. To avoid a labyrinth of foot-

1. In any case, there is some reason to believe that another man, Dr. John Barkham, was largely responsible for Guillim's book *A Display of Heraldrie*.
2. In 1918 a paper by Joan Evans had to be read to the Antiquaries by her brother, then the President. (See f.n. 1 on p. 388 of her *History of the Society of Antiquaries*, 1956.)

notes, the chief biographical sources have been given at the end of each entry, with a few other notes. An attempt has been made to list known manuscripts in the handwriting of each antiquary and to sketch their history, when traceable. The illustrations of handwriting (pp. 140-199) may help in identifying stray anonymous material which turns up, while some of them are interesting.

One cannot hope to have escaped all errors or omissions, and I apologise for them in advance to future users. Local sources of information extensively used include Roland Austin's *Catalogue of the Gloucestershire Collection* (Gloucester Library), the *Bibliographer's Manual of Gloucestershire Literature* and its *Biographical Supplement*, *Gloucestershire Notes and Queries*, the *Transactions* of the Bristol & Gloucestershire Archaeological Society, and Elizabeth Ralph's 'The Society 1876-1976', in *Essays in Bristol and Gloucestershire History* (the centenary volume, 1976). I thank all who have contributed by their willing and helpful replies, verbal and written, to my enquiries, including any who may have been omitted from the following list:

The Librarians and staff of the British Library and Department of Manuscripts, the Bodleian Library, Oxford (particularly Dr. D.M. Barratt and Mr. T.D. Rogers), the Inner Temple, Lincoln's Inn, the Gloucester Library, Cheltenham Library, and Bristol Central Library; Dr. I.H.W. Kenrick of the Historical Manuscript Commission staff, the County Archivist of Gloucestershire (Mr. B.S. Smith)[3] and the City Archivist of Bristol (Miss M.E. Williams) and their staffs; the County Archivists of Berkshire, Cornwall, Kent and West Sussex; the Librarian of Corpus Christi College, Cambridge, the Keeper of the Muniments in the University of St. Andrews, the Keeper of Manuscripts, Fitzwilliam Museum, Cambridge; the Curators of the City of Bristol and Gloucester City Museums; the Royal Institution of Cornwall; the Curator of the Osborn Collection, Yale University Library; the History of Parliament Trust; Mr. Roy Davids of Messrs. Sotheby's; Mr. L.G. Marcus of Messrs George's, Bristol; Mrs. L. Beard, Mr. Tom Bright, Miss S. Eward, Mr. Brian Frith, Dr. Cyril Hart, Mrs. Gwen Hart, Mr. R. Hatchwell, Dr. Nicholas Herbert (Editor, *V.C.H., Glos.*), Mr. A.R. Hobson, Mr. Gerard Leighton, the late Lt. Col. A.B.L. Lloyd-Baker, Mrs. Frances Neale, Miss Elizabeth Ralph, Major L.J.V. Rudder, Mr. G.T. St.J. Sanders, the late Dr. Francis Steer, Mr. D.C.C. Wilson.

3. Now Assistant Secretary of the Historical Manuscripts Commission.

Introduction

Sir Thomas Kendrick, in his engaging little monograph *British Antiquity* (1950), traces with scholarly wit the gradual transmutation of the medieval chronicler, with his obstinate uncritical reliance on tradition and legend, into the modern antiquary and local historian. A typical 'historian' of the Middle Ages was Robert of Gloucester, a shadowy figure who should perhaps be regarded as an ancestor of Gloucestershire antiquaries. His metrical chronicle (University of London MS. 278) was probably completed about the year 1300 in the South Midlands. He seems to have known the town of Gloucester well, and *may* have been a monk of Gloucester Abbey, but the writer of a modern study[1] concludes that the name 'Robert of Gloucester' was first used by John Stow in his *Chronicles of England*, 1586.

Although the old school lingered on even late into the seventeenth century, the new outlook, heralded by John Leland's *Itinerary* (c.1543, though not printed until 1710), was pretty firmly established by the publication of Stow's *Survey of London* in 1598 and of William Camden's *Britannia* in its successive Latin editions from 1586 to 1607, with the English translation of 1610. The early county histories, from Lambarde's *Perambulation of Kent* (1576) to Dugdale's famous *Antiquities of Warwickshire* (1656), reflect the development of practical scholarship, much stimulated by the talented surveyors, mapmakers and topographers, Agas, Saxton, Norden and Speed, and also to some extent by the Heralds, who recorded church monuments and genealogical information in the course of their Visitations.

Such progress, and particularly the publication of its results, would naturally be centred on London and the Home Counties, but Carew's *Survey of Cornwall* (1602) and the work of Devonshire and Welsh antiquaries show that the West Country was by no means in outer darkness. Gloucestershire can scarcely claim to have been in the forefront; it had to wait until the 18th century for a county history. Even the thriving port of Bristol — too commercially minded in its heyday, perhaps — appears to have taken little interest in its history in the 16th and 17th centuries.

---

1. 'Robert of Gloucester's Chronicle', by J.H.P. Pafford, in *Studies presented to Sir Hilary Jenkinson, 1957.*

But Bristol has one earlier pre-eminent claim to distinction, as the birthplace, in 1415, of William Worcestre or Botoner, who has been called 'the first Englishman to deserve the name of antiquary',[2] and 'the first recorded Englishman, whether lay or cleric, to display that particular blend of interests, historical, topographical, and architectural, which has ever since been an outstanding characteristic of the English approach to antiquity.'[3] William Worcestre gives us only a few fleeting glimpses of Gloucestershire in his itineraries, but his elaborate survey of the city of Bristol, as it was in 1480, would alone justify us in saluting him as a founding father of local history. Bristol, too, in its Town Clerk Robert Ricart, had at least one other fifteenth century citizen who —if hardly an antiquary by later standards — showed some concern for recording local happenings from the standpoint of a municipal lawyer. The coincidence of dates and interests is such that Ricart and Worcestre must surely have been acquainted; indeed it is tempting to surmise that Worcestre's Bristol survey of c. 1480 may have been commissioned or suggested by Ricart, who became Town Clerk in 1479.

Samuel Seyer, in his early 19th century *Memoirs of Bristol*,[4] discussed the Bristol manuscript chronicles, of which, he said, probably forty or fifty still remained, chiefly in old Bristol families. One may guess that many of these were copies or adaptations of a few originals, but Seyer himself had seen or used about twenty, 'several written on narrow vellum rolls, one in the City Library, one in possession of Matthew Brickdale,[5] part of one recovered after having been made into a thread-paper, part of another found in the case of a sky-rocket which fell into a garden near my house'. William Adams, the author of a Bristol chronicle nearly a century after Robert Ricart's retirement or death, mentions three earlier ones which he himself had used, naming the writers of two. A perceptive reviewer of *Adams's Chronicle*[6] was of the opinion that Adams had not used Ricart's 'Kalendar', though there was probably some common source for the earlier entries.

Ricart and Adams did not appear in print until 1872 and 1910

2. K.B. McFarlane, 'William Worcester, a Preliminary Survey', in *Studies presented to Sir Hilary Jenkinson*, 1957.
3. John H. Harvey, Introduction to *William Worcestre, Itineraries*, 1969.
4. His Preface, p. x.
5. 1735-1831; M.P. for Bristol.
6. *TBGAS*, xxxiii.

respectively. William Worcestre's *Itineraries* had been printed in the original Latin, not very reliably, in 1778, but Dr. John Harvey's translation was published only in 1969, and this lacks the Bristol survey, on which Mrs. Neale is working.

Meanwhile in rural Gloucestershire antiquaries were emerging. John Smith of Nibley, weaving his story of the Berkeley family, as a labour of love, from about 1600, managed — so he says — to spend 'some parts of each of 34 years' at research in the public records in London, a good two days' journey from Berkeley on horseback. He adds:- 'My travels also and other imployments at home and abroad . . . have bereft me of most of that time which otherwise I had given to this history', and concludes:- 'I only have had the happiness to gather things togeather that were scattered into many corners of this kingdome, and into some parts of forraigne nations, to bring those atcheivements to light that long had lyen in darknes; and to preserve in one body for the after ages of this family what would have been lost . . . .'.[7]

Smith was quite exceptional, but neither he nor another early 17th century pioneer, John Theyer of Brockworth, seems to have had any serious thought of publishing his work. Anthony Wood, the Oxford historian, writing in the third person, gives a lively picture of antiquaries fraternizing at Gloucester in 1668. 'Sept. 1. A.W. went to Cowpers Hill in the company of his acquaintance Timothy Nourse, M.A. & Fellow of University Coll. This Cowpers Hill is a lone-house owned by their acquaintance John Theyer, gent., who had then a very fair library of MSS., reposed in a roome which he had built to retaine them. The next day Mr. Nourse went forward to see some of his relations [while Wood remained, cataloguing manuscripts] . . . Sept. 4. Mr. Nourse returning to us the day before, wee went this day to Glocester, where wee saw the cathedral and monuments therein and several parts of the city; afterwards wee went to the taverne with one or two of the choire, drank a glass of wine and had a song, and so when 'twas neere dark we returned to Coopers Hill'.[8] In December of the same year Wood and Nourse foregathered with Theyer at an Oxford tavern, and no doubt it was through his acquaintanceship with Nourse that Theyer sent his son Charles to University College, his own college having been Magdalen.

7. *Lives of the Berkeleys*, II, 440, 443.
8. *The Life & Times of Anthony Wood of Oxford*, 1632-1692, described by himself, ed. A. Clark, 1891-1900, Vol. II, 143.

When Timothy Nourse 'went forward', it must have been to Newent, beyond the Severn, where the Nourse family lived. Timothy (d. 1699) was a numismatist and a writer on husbandry, etc. Some interesting notes of 1707 on the history of Newent[9] were made by his brother, Walter Nourse (?1654-1742) or perhaps by the latter's son, also Walter, who died in 1711, aged 24. In the later seventeenth century the ecclesiastical lawyer Richard Parsons (1643-1711) evidently had ideas of writing a county history, but his health failing he resigned his claim to Sir Robert Atkyns. It cannot have been until Atkyns retired from politics after the accession of William III in 1689 that he really turned his attention to the history of Gloucestershire. In fact the first to publish proposals for such a project, in 1685, was neither a country gentleman nor a cleric, but the parish clerk of St. John's church, Gloucester, Abel Wantner, whose completed history, of considerable merit, remains in manuscript in the Bodleian Library.

Although we know strangely little about Sir Robert Atkyns, considering that he was a county magnate, a Member of Parliament, and the son of an eminent judge, it is evident that he was able to spend time on research into archives in London, for which his legal training equipped him; and there are indications that much of his local research was done by proxy, rather than by circularizing informants, as Rudder and others did later. His *Ancient and Present State of Glostershire*, not published until 1712, the year after his death, also owed a good deal to the labours of Richard Parsons.[10] If Atkyns's book lacks human interest and he has been criticized, e.g. by John Prinn and later by Samuel Seyer, for failing to quote his sources,[11] it should be remembered that it was one of the earlier county histories[12] and that several of the well-known ones (Hasted's *Kent*, Nash's *Worcestershire*, Morant's *Essex*, Manning's *Surrey*, and others) were not published until nearly a century later.

Of four Gloucestershire antiquaries who flourished in the early eighteenth century, not one left anything in print, though three

9. G.R.O., D412 Z3 and D1810/13. For the family, see *Visitation of Glos., 1682-3*.
10. See no. 7.
11. In Prinn's letter to Ballard quoted on p. 53, he remarks : "Our author has done his work no credit by concealing the authorities for all he wrote". Seyer (preface to his *Memoirs of Bristol*) says of Atkyns: "Unfortunately it is not his practice to quote authorities".
12. Cf. W.G. Hoskins, *Local History in England*, pp. 16-19.

had made substantial collections and drafts. John Prinn (1661-1735), a Cheltenham lawyer, seems to have preserved and transcribed documents without much intention of writing for publication; Richard Graves, the squire of Mickleton (1677-1729), died before he had begun a long-contemplated history of the Vale of Evesham; Richard Furney (1694-1753), a native and parish priest of Gloucester, who became Archdeacon of Surrey, left numerous manuscripts including an unpublished Gloucestershire history; and George Ballard (1706-1755) was rather a collector of antiquities than a writer. Graves, Furney and Ballard were all correspondents of the Oxford antiquary and librarian Thomas Hearne (1678-1735), and letters of all three to Hearne, with at least one from John Prinn to Ballard, are in the Bodleian Library, — a valuable source for Gloucestershire antiquarian studies of the period. It was evidently Graves who introduced Ballard to Hearne, for he writes on February 21st, 1726/7: '. . . I was willing to embrace this opportunity of writing to you by the bearer, who is the young tailor of Campden I told you of, that he's collected so many old coins &c . . . whose name is George Ballard.'[13]

Until the mid-eighteenth century, when turnpike roads and stage-coaches had become widespread, travelling was so slow and arduous that except in London and the university towns the antiquary had to work very much in isolation, though communication by post was surprisingly good from at any rate the later seventeen-hundreds. Both Graves and Furney, for instance, corresponded with Browne Willis (1682-1760),[14] whose surveys of English abbeys (1715) and cathedrals (1727) included Gloucestershire and Bristol. Willis helped to organize the present Society of Antiquaries of London in 1717, but few of the remoter provincial antiquaries could have derived much benefit from the Society in its earlier years. The first of ours to be elected a Fellow appears to have been William Barrett, the historian of Bristol, in 1775. He can have taken little if any part in the Antiquaries' proceedings. The ephemeral Elizabethan Society of Antiquaries, which was presumably founded about 1586 and faded away about 1608,[15] must have been almost exclusively a London coterie. It was not until the 19th century that men of kindred interests in

13. Bodl., Rawlinson lett. 6.
14. Letters in Bodl., Willis 43.
15. Joan Evans, *A History of the Society of Antiquaries* (1956), pp. 8-13.

history and archaeology were able to fraternize (or bicker) freely in local antiquarian societies.

Fifty years after Atkyns's death, two men differing widely in their background and predilections were each concocting a history of Gloucestershire. Both were assiduous workers. Ralph Bigland, born in 1711, was of a good north-country family but married into Gloucestershire; in his forties he became a Herald, and eventually Garter King of Arms. His history was originally to have been a revision of Atkyns's, but as he was forestalled by the appearance of Rudder's *New History* in 1779, he decided to concentrate on genealogy and heraldry and to make his book 'rather more a history of the inhabitants than of the shire itself'.[16] Bigland's great merit is to have recorded and preserved from the vandalism of 19th century church 'restoration' great numbers of monumental inscriptions in Gloucestershire churches. Dying in 1784 he left his work unfinished, to be published piecemeal during the next hundred years. Samuel Rudder, born in 1726, was a self-educated countryman who became a printer in Cirencester. His *New History of Gloucestershire* chiefly brought Atkyns up to date, but his contemporary notes and lively comments add a good deal of human colour. He too was forestalled — by the second (unrevised) edition of Atkyns's history, 1768 — but he persevered, and published in 1779.

In Bristol not an antiquary stirs for a century or more after William Adams's chronicle ends, about 1640. At length, half way through the 18th century, we find a medical practitioner, William Barrett, struggling in his spare time, and after early retirement, to write the story of his city, by then second only to London in population and as a port.[17] He finishes a very creditable pioneer effort, and it appears in 1789, the year of his death. His young friend and more scholarly successor, the Reverend Samuel Seyer (1775-1831) produces thirty-five years later his *Memoirs . . . of Bristol and its neighbourhood*. Meanwhile interest has been aroused by Barrett's book. In 1816 there appears a popular *History of Bristol*, of which John Evans, a schoolmaster and Nonconformist preacher, is part author. William Tyson (1785-1851), editor of the Bristol Times and Mirror, makes a feature of local history in his paper and collects material for another history

16. Letter to the Rev. H.G. Dobyns-Yate, 1 Jan. 1780 (G.R.O., Pc 179).
17. Cf. Brian Smith and Elizabeth Ralph, *A History of Bristol and Gloucestershire* (1972), Chap. XVIII.

of Bristol, which he never writes. And the Rev. James Dallaway (1763-1834), a Gloucestershire man and considerable scholar, publishes among his many works one entitled *Antiquities of Bristow in the Middle Centuries*. Decidedly Bristol is now on the historical map.

Let us return to Gloucestershire. I have not so far had occasion to use the word archaeology. Field archaeology had its tentative beginnings with such men as John Aubrey in the 17th century and Stukeley in the early 18th; and serious excavation was undertaken in Kent and Wiltshire later in the 18th century.[18] A contemporary of William Cunnington and his patron and collaborator Sir Richard Colt Hoare in Wiltshire was Samuel Lysons, senior (1763-1819), surely the greatest of Gloucestershire antiquaries. Lysons took a leading part in the affairs of the Society of Antiquaries as their Director and later Vice-President; he also collaborated with his brother Daniel, the Rector of Rodmarton in Gloucestershire, in an ambitious topographical survey of England, *Magna Britannia*, which was abandoned after Samuel died, at the height of his powers, aged 56. His excavations in Gloucestershire, notably of the great Woodchester Villa, laid the foundations for later study of Romano-British life in the Cotswolds.

The eighteenth century was the age of the great folio county histories. With the spread of education and the improvement in communications, there was by 1800 a market for something handier in format, and this was supplied for both the county and the city of Gloucester by two more historians, both local clergymen. Thomas Rudge, afterwards Archdeacon of Gloucester and author of a survey of Gloucestershire agriculture, modestly offered his books of 1803 and 1811 as an up-to-date version of Atkyns and Rudder. T.D. Fosbroke, a hard-working scholar with a perpetual grievance against the world, wrote in September 1818 to Nichols, his publisher, who had issued printed *Proposals* for his own well-researched history of Gloucester City: 'I absolutely did not know, till a week or two ago . . . that Archdeacon Rudge had published a thin octavo of scissors-and-paste compilation in 1811'.[19] The two were unfortunate, as Bigland and Rudder had been, in finding themselves in competition for a still limited public. Ten years after Fosbroke's, another small but useful

18. See Professor R.J.C. Atkinson's Introduction to the biography of William Cunnington (1754-1810), *From Antiquary to Archaeologist*, 1975.
19. *TBGAS*, xxxvii, 150.

history of the city was produced by a Gloucester attorney, George Worrall Counsel.

Well-off amateur historians active in the early 19th century, principally as collectors of antiquities, included John Delafield Phelps of Chavenage and George Weare Braikenridge, of a Bristol merchant family. The awkward social relations between a wealthy dilettante like Braikenridge and a journalist of humbler origins, William Tyson, are amusingly revealed in correspondence from both angles.[20] In 1830 the topographer John Britton (himself, incidentally, a self-made man) had evidently offered to put up Tyson for the Fellowship of the Antiquaries, and Braikenridge, a Fellow since 1827, had been asked to support the proposal. Braikenridge seems to have been kindly disposed, though perhaps rather pompous. But Tyson, in a letter to Britton, writes : 'It is extremely unpleasant to me to enter upon the subject of the Antiquarian Society. I return to you the certificate you last sent me because . . . I consider that it might afford room to the other gentlemen to object to it . . . Mr. Braikenridge is such a matter-of-fact man that I have no doubt he would even demur to the substitution of the word Esq. instead of Mr. in my description.' Braikenridge had, however, written to Britton, of Tyson: '. . . I am perfectly convinced we have not in this City a more zealous antiquary than he is.' At any rate, the election went through.

Two local historians whose books have stood the test of time are James Bennett, printer and bookseller (*History of Tewkesbury*, 1830, reprinted 1976) and Paul Hawkins Fisher (*Notes & Recollections of Stroud*, published in his extreme old age, 1871, and reprinted 1975). Several antiquaries born between 1780 and 1800 are of more than local repute. George Ormerod, the historian of Cheshire, migrated in mid-life to Tidenham in the Forest of Dean and studied the antiquities of his new home. Contrariwise, the Rev. H.T. Ellacombe — an authority on church bells — after 33 years at Bitton near Bristol became Rector of a Devon parish, and wrote the history of both. Another cleric, Samuel Roffey Maitland, grandfather of the famous constitutional historian Frederick Maitland, went from Gloucester to be librarian of Lambeth Palace. Lastly, the celebrated collector of books and manuscripts, Sir Thomas Phillipps, started life on the Gloucestershire border near Broadway and

20. Bris.L.,22992.

ended it at Thirlestane House in Cheltenham, where he had latterly stored his mammoth collection.

As it chances, none of our antiquaries was born between 1792 and 1809. We now come, therefore, to a generation born between 1810 and 1830, many of whom lived until nearly the end of the century and were concerned in the founding (1876) and formative years of the Bristol & Gloucestershire Archaeological Society. None, except Sir John Maclean, was of more than local note, but it is well to be reminded of the sterling if unspectacular work that these Victorians did for history and archaeology in Bristol and Gloucestershire.

Sir John Maclean retired from London to the Forest of Dean in 1871; an archaeologist (mainly in Cornwall) as well as expert in historical archives, he helped to found the 'B. and G.' and played a leading role in its activities for a number of years. J.D.T. Niblett, a collector of Gloucestershire books, had ideas of writing a new county history, but they came to nothing. John Goding wrote the first serious history of Cheltenham, and the Rev. H.G. Nicholls the first history of the Forest of Dean. Another country parson, David Royce, was a retiring scholar who collected flint implements and coins and spent many years in editing the Winchcombe Cartulary.

In Victorian Bristol those chiefly known as antiquaries and local historians were the City Librarian, John Taylor, a journalist, John Latimer, two booksellers, Thomas Kerslake and William George, and a city alderman, Francis Fox. Only Taylor and Fox were Bristol-born; George came from Dunster in Somerset, Kerslake from Exeter, and Latimer from Newcastle-on-Tyne. Still more surprisingly, an Irish clergyman with the curious name of Beaver Blacker, who lived latterly at Clifton, had transferred his affections from Dublin to Gloucestershire when over fifty; working like the proverbial beaver his namesake, he contributed constantly to *Notes & Queries*, and founded and for twelve years ran the very successful *Gloucestershire N. & Q.*, which is still a mine of local information a century later.

The nineteenth century saw the end of comparative isolation for the antiquary. An attempt soon after 1840 to start a county archaeological society[21] proved abortive, but the Cotteswold

---

21. This paragraph is largely condensed from Elizabeth Ralph's 'The Society 1876-1976', in *Essays in Bristol and Gloucestershire History*, the Society's Centenary Volume, pp. 2-5.

Naturalists' Field Club, founded in 1846, soon developed an 'archaeological group'. In 1874 John Taylor read to the British Archaeological Association, which had chosen Bristol for its Meeting that year, a paper on the history and architecture of the area. The interest aroused, it seems, inspired local antiquaries to unite (Somerset and Wiltshire already had societies), and after preliminary discussions the Bristol and Gloucestershire Archaeological Society was established at a meeting held in Bristol on 21 April 1876. A provisional committee had already recruited over 400 prospective members, among them well-known people in the county and in Bristol, with Sir William Guise as first President. A focus was at last provided for antiquarian interests, and for the next hundred years, with a gradually growing membership, the Society has continued to foster them.

Although it constantly promoted lectures, visited sites, and published reports on archaeological subjects, the Society did little in the way of excavation until the end of the century. This was perhaps just as well, for amateurish 'opening' of prehistoric barrows, which was done now and then as a demonstration for field meetings, has since been regretted.[22] The Cotswold barrows had long attracted notice. As early as 1821 Hetty Pegler's Tump in Uley was investigated by Dr. Fry for T.J. Lloyd-Baker, F.S.A., and again in 1854 by the Wiltshire craniologist Dr. John Thurnam. Members of the Cotteswold Field Club, including Canon Samuel Lysons, excavated various tumuli between 1850 and 1880, including the Nympsfield Long Barrow. The well-known Belas Knap was explored, after a fashion, in 1863-65. Excavation of several more barrows was carried out between 1867 and 1876 by the Rev. David Royce, and between 1880 and 1884 by G.B. Witts, a civil and railway engineer, who also published in 1883 an *Archaeological Handbook of Gloucestershire*. But scientific digging was still in its infancy, and has only reached years of discretion in the present century.

Gloucestershire is also rich in Roman villas. Samuel Lysons, senior, had excavated in 1794 the palatial mansion at Woodchester and in 1818 the Witcombe villa. The well-known Chedworth villa was investigated in 1864 but not by local talent. The first villa excavation sponsored by the Archaeological

22. Helen O'Neil and L.V. Grinsell, *Gloucestershire Barrows*, (*TBGAS* lxxix), p. 58.

Society was the one at Tockington, near Bristol, in 1887; little else of this kind was done before the turn of the century. The Cotteswold Field Club has continued to flourish, but concerning itself by degrees less with archaeology than with natural history and geology. Since 1876 the story of Gloucestershire and Bristol antiquaries has been largely that of the 'B. & G.', which has given so many enthusiasts not only the fellowship of others, but a means of publishing the results of their own work, whether historical or archaeological. Canon William Bazeley was secretary from 1879 to 1907, Sir John Maclean editor of the Society's *Transactions* from 1878 to 1894, Canon C.S. Taylor editor 1894-96 and 1899-1914, and Roland Austin secretary 1917-28 and 1937-44, and editor 1923-49. All wrote many papers for the *Transactions*. Maclean also edited John Smith's 17th century 'Berkeley Manuscripts', Taylor wrote *An Analysis of the Domesday of Gloucestershire*, while F.A. (later Sir Francis) Hyett, an authority on Gloucestershire books, collaborated with Bazeley in the *Bibliographer's Manual of Gloucestershire Literature*, and with Austin, twenty years later, in its *Biographical Supplement*. All these and other 'occasional publications' of the Society have been of lasting value as reference books.

Several of the mid-Victorian antiquaries lived on well into the present century, while general interest in local studies grew continuously. Their own interests were varied. W.P.W. Phillimore (1853-1913), a genealogist and expert on records, was of Gloucestershire descent but became known nationally. F.S. Hockaday (1855-1924), with phenomenal industry, opened to students the Gloucester Diocesan Archives, previously almost unexplored. W. St. Clair Baddeley (1856-1946) was an enthusiast both in local history and in excavation. W.H. Knowles (1857-1943), coming to Gloucestershire from Newcastle when already 65, was yet able to leave to the county an outstanding legacy of architectural history. He too excavated, but in the period between the two wars field archaeology, increasingly sophisticated, was being undertaken for the most part either by experts from the Ancient Monuments Department and elsewhere, or by younger archaeologists like Dr. Dobson-Hinton and Mrs. Clifford, whose lives do not fall within the scope of this book. Our last antiquary is Roland Austin, who after thirty years as Gloucester City Librarian became the first County Records Officer, and whose long and dedicated membership of the Bristol

& Gloucestershire Archaeological Society covered almost the first half of the twentieth century.

Here this survey ends. The 'antiquary' has always been essentially an amateur, — that is, he does it for the love of the thing. The increasing professionalism of academics and archaeologists has not made amateurs an anachronism; instead, they grow more numerous and their interests more varied. Some of them have attained to professional standards; and the professionals, if they are worth their salt, are also amateurs in their spare time. It might be invidious to mention the living, but of those who were still with us in recent years, such names as Elsie Clifford, Will Croome, Joan Evans, Dina Dobson-Hinton, H.P.R. Finberg, E.S. Lindley and Stewart Gracie will remind all who knew them that Gloucestershire and Bristol can still take pride in antiquaries not less gifted, nor less memorable as personalities, than those of the more distant past.

ANTIQUARIES
OF
GLOUCESTERSHIRE
AND BRISTOL

1. William WORCESTRE alias BOTONER, 1415 - c. 1485

William Worcestre, who sometimes used his mother's surname of Botoner instead of his patronymic — at times also with the unexplained letters H R above his signature — was the son of William (de) Worcestre, a respectable burgess and whittawer (saddler) of Bristol, and his wife Elizabeth Botoner, of a prominent Coventry and Bristol family.[1] A Scholar of Great Hart Hall, Oxon., by 1432, William junior was secretary (c. 1438 - 59) to Sir John Fastolf, the Agincourt veteran, ex-Regent of Normandy, and Norfolk magnate. As such he figures in the Paston letters, some of which are in his hand. He undertook various journeys on his master's business, and for many years after Fastolf's death in 1459 Worcestre, as an executor, remained involved with his complicated affairs. He was living at Pockthorpe, on the outskirts of Norwich, in his later years, and was dead by 1485.

By 1449 Worcestre "had begun to form antiquarian collections .... It was his normal practice not only to mention his authority for a statement, but also the date and place at which he learnt it."[2] On August 17th, 1478, in his sixties, he rode off from Norfolk on an antiquarian pilgrimage to St. Michael's Mount in Cornwall, via London, Southampton and Bristol, with an excursion across the Severn to Tintern Abbey; he returned with some variations in the route, to London, which he reached on October the 8th. In 1480 he journeyed from Norwich to London and through Oxford, Cirencester and Bristol to Wells and Glastonbury.

The unique manuscript of William Worcestre's 'Itineraries' contains his diaries of these travels, with copious notes recorded from his own observation or what others told him, chiefly of topographical features and of the churches and religious houses which he visited. Besides his general curiosity about local tradition and legend, and about books and manuscripts, he displays particular interest in architecture, which he often records in accurate detail almost unknown in other writers of his period. The manuscript includes many miscellaneous historical memoranda and pieces of undigested information relating to Norfolk and elsewhere, but its most valuable section — originally a separate sheaf of notes now bound up with the rest — is his detailed survey of the city of

Bristol, street by street.

The Itineraries remained almost unknown until published, in their original Latin, by James Nasmith in 1778 and reprinted by James Dallaway in 1834.[3] They have recently been edited much more fully, with an English translation, by Dr. John H. Harvey, F.S.A. (see below), whose qualifications as both architectural historian and archivist made him peculiarly fitted for the strenuous task of interpreting Worcestre's hasty and crabbed fifteenth century script, some of it doubtless written on horseback. The Bristol survey was not included in Dr. Harvey's book and is now being translated and edited, to complement it, by Mrs. Frances Neale.[4]

Publications (none in the writer's lifetime): James Nasmith, *Itineraria Symonis Simeonis et Willelmi de Worcestre*, 1778; James Dallaway, *Antiquities of Bristow in the Middle Centuries, including the topography by William Worcestre* ....,1834; John H. Harvey, *William Worcestre: Itineraries*, 1969 (less the Bristol survey); F. Neale, *William Worcestre: Bristol* (forthcoming).

MSS. Corpus Christi College, Cambridge, MS 210 is the original and only autograph manuscript of William Worcestre's 'Itineraries'. Presumably with its author when he died, at Norwich, it has later entries in other hands, two of which have been identified as those of Robert Talbot, a prebendary of Norwich (c.1505 - 1558) and Henry Aldrich, a Fellow of Corpus Christi, Cambridge, who was licensed to teach grammar in Norwich in 1583. Through him, most likely, the MS. was acquired by the College.[5]

Odd notes and letters of William Worcestre are in the British Library (Paston Letters, Add.43488 - 91, and other collections), the Norfolk Record Office, at Magdalen College, Oxford and elsewhere. The *Boke of Noblesse* (Lambeth Palace MS. 506) is pretty well established by the late Dr. K.B. McFarlane to be by Worcestre. Two of his antiquarian works are now lost, the 'Antiquitates Anglie' and the 'De Agri Norfolcensis familiis antiquis', the latter still surviving in the 17th century.

Biographical Sources: D.N.B.; F.A. (Cardinal) Gasquet, 'The note books of William Worcester, a fifteenth century antiquary', in *The Old English Bible and other Essays*, 1897; Sir Thomas Kendrick, *British Antiquity*, 1950, pp. 29 - 33; K.B. McFarlane, 'William Worcester: a Preliminary Survey', in *Studies presented to Hilary Jenkinson*, 1957; John H. Harvey, *William Worcestre:*

Itineraries, 1969, and 'William Worcestre: A Clarification', in the *Genealogists' Magazine*, June 1970.

Notes.
1. *Itineraries* (ed. J.H. Harvey), p. 311.
2. K.B. McFarlane, 'William Worcester, a Preliminary Survey', see Biographical sources.
3. With some additional inaccuracies. Meanwhile Ralph Bigland, in his Gloucestershire history, had briefly quoted Worcestre, going back to the original MS. to improve on Nasmith. See *Itineraries* (ed. Harvey), Introduction, p. xxii.
4. I am particularly grateful to Mrs. Neale for suggesting some improvements to these notes on Worcestre.
5. See *Itineraries* (ed. Harvey), Introduction, pp. xix-xx.

2. Robert RICART, fl. 1466 - 1508

Among early archives of our ancient cities and boroughs there are sometimes to be found custumals or remembrance books, compiled as a 'corporate memory' to which reference could be made for laws and customs affecting local government. Occasionally an enterprising Town Clerk or other official would expand such a record into a chronicle of local events.[1]

Robert Ricart, whose dates of birth and death have not been traced, was vestry clerk of All Saints' church, Bristol for twelve years, and then, in 1479, was elected Town Clerk of the city, an office which he held for at least twenty-seven years at a salary of £4 a year, plus allowances for parchment, wax, wine, and fur for his gown. His handwriting is found in the Little Red Book of Bristol until 1508, and he was succeeded as Town Clerk by Philip Ricart, doubtless a son or near relative. Robert Ricart is said to have been a member of the Gild of Kalendars, a fraternity attached to All Saints', which maintained a school and a library, but the 19th century editor of his chronicle could find no evidence to confirm this, or the statement that Ricart's will left benefactions to the church and fraternity. (See Note 2 below, however).

'The Maire of Bristowe is Kalendar', which was printed by the Camden Society in 1872, is written mostly in Ricart's own hand. He tells us that it was compiled at the command of William Spencer, who was Mayor when he became Town Clerk; and on folio 153a (page 68 in the printed volume) he records: "I, Robert Ricart, Towne Clerke of Bristowe, have made and devised this present boke for a remembratif, to be called the Maire of Bristowe is Regestre or elles the Maires Kallendre." The book is divided into six parts, of which the first two are concerned with national history, culled from earlier chronicles including Matthew Paris's 13th century Flores Historiarum. Parts 4 to 6 give the laws, ordinances and customs of Bristol in great detail. The third part contains annual entries of the names of the Mayor and councillors, with the main events, national and local, during their term of office, but this chronicle, which has been continued to the present day, is unfortunately omitted between 1497 and 1522. As it is an official record, personal sidelights such as are found in William Adams's later chronicle cannot be expected. The most striking features are the pictorial plan of Bristol and the lively painting (as a frontispiece to Part 4) which shows a new Mayor taking the oath of office in St. George's chapel in the Bristol Guildhall, surrounded by the city aldermen and officers including the Town Clerk, who is administering the oath. This is presumably intended to be Ricart, who may also have been the artist.

Ricart's chronicle, of course, was scarcely the work of an antiquary, but it proved useful to later Bristol historians including Samuel Seyer. In the 16th century it had come to the notice of the itinerant antiquary John Leland, who described it as "a little boke of the antiquities of the House of Calendaries in Brightstow".[2] It was also used by John Smith of Nibley.[3]

Publication: *The Maire of Bristowe is Kalendar*, ed. Lucy Toulmin Smith (Camden Soc., n.s. V), 1872.

MS. B.R.O., 04720, Bristol Corporation Archives: The Maires Kalendar. A folio vol. of 332 paper leaves, much rubricated, interspersed in places with parchment leaves, some of them used for illuminated drawings, which include a plan of Bristol, scene of Mayor's oath-taking (see above) and a number of 'portraits' of English kings.

Biographical sources: *D.N.B.*: L. Toulmin Smith, *Introduction* to Camden Soc. edn. of *The Maires Kalendar* (see above); *Guide to the Bristol Archives Office* (1971), p.3; Elizabeth Ralph, 'Robert Ricart', in *St. Stephen's* (Bristol) *Review*, May 1962.

Notes. 1. From which a local history might later be compiled, e.g. the *Annalls of Ipswiche*, 1649, by the Borough Recorder, Nathaniel Bacon.
2. The editor of the Maires Kalendar identifies it with confidence as the book Leland saw, because he quotes passages from it verbatim. The title must have made him associate it with the Bristol Kalendars' Gild, and this may have originated the tradition that Ricart was a member of the Gild.
3. See his *Lives of the Berkeleys* (1883), II, 447.

3. John SMITH ('Smith of Nibley'), 1567 - 1641

Of all the antiquaries of Bristol and Gloucestershire there is none whose personality comes through to us more vividly in his writings than Smith of Nibley's. His attractive, humorous character, no less than his achievements as a local historian much in advance of his time, cry out for a full-length biographer.

Like William Worcestre, John Smith[1] led a busy life in the service of a landowning family, though the Berkeleys, unlike Worcestre's master Sir John Fastolf, were ancient nobility. Smith did not come from Gloucestershire; he was the son of a Leicestershire gentleman and from 1584 was a page and companion to Thomas[2], son and heir of Henry, 17th Lord Berkeley, at the Berkeley seat of Callowden in Warwickshire. He accompanied Thomas to Magdalen College, Oxford, afterwards studying law at the Middle Temple. Becoming in 1596 household steward at Berkeley Castle and in 1597 steward of the Hundred and Liberty of Berkeley, Smith gave faithful service to the Berkeley family for more than fifty years, and left to posterity a unique history of the family. His home was at North Nibley, between Berkeley and Wotton-under-Edge.

Though elected to Parliament for Midhurst in 1621, doubtless by Berkeley influence, John Smith took no further part in politics, but was active in the affairs of the Virginia Company and the foundation of the Berkeley Plantation on the James River, Virginia, by Gloucestershire colonists in 1619.[3] He died on the eve of the Civil War, after finishing in December 1639 his *History of the Hundred of Berkeley*, which with the *Lives of the Berkeleys* is his monument. Neither was to be printed in full for nearly two and a half centuries, though some later historians were aware of their value. The MS. *Lives* was used by Dugdale in his *Baronage of England* (1675 - 6), but thereafter neglected until T.D. Fosbroke printed extracts in 1821. Following a paper by J.H. Cooke, F.S.A., in volume V of the Bristol & Gloucestershire Archaeological Society's *Transactions* (1881), Sir John Maclean edited the complete 'Berkeley Manuscripts' (i.e. the *Lives* and the *Hundred of Berkeley*) for the Society, only a few years after its foundation.

Smith's muster roll of 'all the able and sufficient men .... within the County of Gloucester ....' (1608), compiled for the 17th Baron Berkeley as Lord Lieutenant, was published in 1902 — almost an early 17th century county directory, with its invaluable details of age, occupation, physical fitness, and arms.

Fosbroke may have exaggerated when he compared John Smith's erudition to the great William Dugdale's, but Smith himself, in his characteristic prologue to the *Lives of the Berkeleys* (where he says modestly: "In a playne and home-bred stile ....Ile freely write the truth I knowe") tells of his forty years of research in original records, then so hard of access, — not only the "vast fields" of the family archives, but "the King's severall Courts, desolated monasteries, the private stores of more than fourscore men, with an hundred other manuscripts and chartularies". After a further long and picturesque catalogue of his sources, he concludes: "Where still remaine many fragrant and faire flowers .... And my grave shall bless that foot that walketh after them, and that hand that picks them up and bundles them with these."

His other work, *The Hundred of Berkeley*, shows how wide and modern were Smith's interests, extending to folk-lore, dialect, place-names (though he is often mistaken over derivations), agriculture, the Severn with its fisheries, and even anthropology.[4] And as the archivist of the Berkeley family, he claimed that "by the happiness of my poore endeavors, more than 300 pieces of evidence have been returned into their evidence house from many corners."

Publications: *The Berkeley Manuscripts* (*Lives of the Berkeleys*, 2 vols. and *The Hundred of Berkeley*, 1 vol.) ed. Sir John Maclean, 1883 - 85; *Men & Armour for Gloucestershire in 1608* (compiled by John Smith), 1902.

MSS. 1. The Osborn Collection, Yale Univy. Library, U.S.A., has (ref. a 22) an early manuscript volume in Smith's writing, containing Latin commentaries on Greek and Hebrew texts, as well as the Lord's Prayer and Apostles' Creed in Italian and French. This shows the extent of his education. On the dorse of folio 1 there is a later signed note by Smith, in Latin, dating the book as 'about 11 Nov. 1599 and in his 32nd year'.

2. Also in the Osborn Collection (ref. fb 151) is a copy of the *Lives of the Berkeleys*, c. 1628 (3 vols.) transcribed by 'J.A.', some verses by whom are appended. This MS. came to Yale from Mr.

Richard Hatchwell, who bought it at Sothebys on 26 June 1967 (lot 586) from the Phillipps Collection. It bears the bookplate of Sir Francis Fust, Bt. (d.1769), of Hill Court near Berkeley, was sold at Hill Court in 1846 (see *N. & Q.*, ser. 1, v. 616) to Mr. Smith-Pigott of Brockley, and acquired by Sir Thomas Phillipps at the Smith-Pigott sale of 1849.

3. On finishing his Hundred of Berkeley, John Smith bade farewell to "all my 20 other bookes, the recreations of my last 50 years."[5] A list of actually 21 volumes follows, comprising the Berkeley Lives (3 vols.), Hundred of Berkeley (1 vol.), 'Men & Armour, 1608' (3 vols.), Glos. Lieutenancy Minutes, 1-11 Jas. I (1 vol.), and various local and Berkeley estate records. Some of these, including the Berkeley MSS. and Hundred of Berkeley, are still among the Berkeley Castle muniments, but 'Men & Armour' descended in the Smith family and was bought at the Quaritch sale in 1888 (see below) by Lord Sherborne, who allowed it to be published in 1902. It is now deposited in the G.R.O. (ref. D 678). None of these MSS. is likely to be in the handwriting of John Smith himself, but some may be copies made by his son or by his confidential clerk William Archard (see below under *Biographical sources*), to whom jointly he dedicated his Hundred of Berkeley as "in many sallies abroad and serches at home my helpers and amanuenses". He says, in fact, that the three volumes of the Lives of the Berkeleys were "lately copied out by one of you."[6]

A further list of five volumes, making 26 in all, follows the list of twenty-one. These are called: (1) "That of my life, in quarto", (2) a History of the Borough & Manor of Tetbury, (3) History of the Manor & Hundred of Bosham, Sussex, (4) History of the Honour & Manor of Melton Mowbray, (5) History of Bitton, Glos.; "of all of which I have been Steward", says Smith. These five books have apparently disappeared, but there are drafts of three of the local histories, nos. 2 — 4, in the British Library (see 4 below). Smith's autobiography would be of great interest, if it could be found.

4. The late E.S. Lindley, F.S.A. (see below) traced in considerable detail the story of John Smith's personal papers and documents and their tangled connection with the Berkeley muniments, which suffered depredations to an unknown extent after the Civil War siege of the Castle. Briefly, the Smith family papers were handed down through the Smiths, Smythes, Smythe-Owens and Owens to Reginald Cholmondeley of Condover Hall, Salop, a property which had come into the family through the

marriage of Nicholas Smythe in 1767. Nicholas moved to Shropshire, taking the records with him. When Reginald Cholmondeley's manuscripts were reported on by the Historical MSS. Commission in their 5th Report of 1876, they consisted mainly of John Smith the antiquary's documents, letters and papers, including a "well-filled volume of notes made by Mr. Smith while he sat in Parliament". (For this see below). All this collection was sold at auction by Puttick & Simpson in 1887 and resold by Bernard Quaritch in 1888 or soon after. Their later history is summarized in the *Glos. Coll. Catalogue* (see below); the papers relating to Virginia, etc.[7] went to the New York Public Library, while a large Gloucestershire section was bought by F.A. Crisp, F.S.A. and acquired from his executor by the Gloucester City Library, where most of them are bound in sixteen volumes (Glos. Coll. 13605) but some are under other references. Others were dispersed. One group, acquired by the British Library, is now B.L. Add. 33588 and 33589. The latter concerns almost entirely later generations of the Smith family, but 33588 includes papers and correspondence of John Smith (1567 - 1641) and amongst them are an imperfect draft of his life of Maurice, 8th Lord Berkeley and brief draft histories of the Berkeley manors of Tetbury, Glos.; Bosham, Sussex; Seagrave, Leics.; Callowden, Warws. and Melton Mowbray, Leics. Presumably these were fair-copied or written up later, as Smith would hardly have referred to the drafts as 'books' in his list quoted in para. 3 above.

Also in the British Library, MS. Add. 34121 is Smith's autograph diary of the House of Commons proceedings of 1621, when he sat as a member for Midhurst.

Biographical sources: *D.N.B.*; Sir John Maclean, Prefaces to Vols. I and III of the *Berkeley Manuscripts*, 1883, 1885; J.H. Cooke, 'The Berkeley Manuscripts and their Author', in *TBGAS*, v. 212-221; *Hist. MSS. Commn., 5th Report* (1876), pt. 1, 333-360; *Bulletin of the New York Public Library*, July 1897, i, 186-90; *Glos. Coll. Cat.*, 2122 etc, 13605, 13620 etc.; E.S. Lindley, 'William Archard', in *TBGAS*, lxviii, 190-198, and 'A John Smyth Bibliography', in *TBGAS*, lxxx, 121-31; Irvine Gray, 'Smith of Nibley's Will', in *TBGAS*, lxxviii, 129-136.

Notes. 1. The name has often been printed Smyth. In the 16th and 17th centuries i and y were interchangeable, but there can be no doubt that the historian called himself Smith, as

indeed he usually wrote his name, e.g. in his Will and on the title-page of the Lives of the Berkeleys. It also appears as Smith in the Heralds' Visitations of 1623 and 1682/3, though 18th century descendants adopted the affectation of 'Smythe'.
2. This Thomas died before his father.
3. See 'Berkeley Plantation, Virginia', by Canon J.E. Gethyn-Jones, M.B.E., F.S.A., in *TBGAS*, xciv, 5-17.
4. e.g. on p. 329: "In this parish Slimbridge hathe longe continued the family of the Knights, men of meane ranke, of whom 4 lineall generations of well proportioned men are remembered to have had five fingers and a thumbe on each hand."
5. *Hundred of Berkeley*, pp. 411-412.
6. Ibid., p. 34.
7. Most of them printed in S.M. Kingsbury's *Records of the Virginia Company of London*, (1933), vol. 3.

4. William ADAMS, c. 1585 - c. 1650

A source of some value for early Bristol history is the chronicle "written in Bristol by William Addames *in anno* 1625", to which is added a record of current events for about fourteen years. The preamble 'To the Reader' tells us a little of the author and might serve as a precept to others.

"Many are the causes that incyted me to write this booke before I had resolved to take the paines: first, at a time of two years leisure I had read much and kept some privat notes thereof, then considering that much reading but littell availeth in a Commonwealth without participating of some records thereof unto posteritie. Secondly, I penned the same for my delight and helpe of memory, without which all reading is but a hidden talent. Thirdly, to stop the mowthes of foolish people, that will talke what a merry world it was in former ages, when (poore soules) they know not what they say."

For his entry for the year 1264[1] we learn something of his local sources:

"I have been a little troubled until I came to this place, having 3 books of several mens writing before me, and each of them differed in sundry places between [the years] 1237 and 1264 .... one book that was Phillip Jenkens, a coroner of our city, began King Henry III's reign in 1215; another *in anno* 1216, which is right; and the third written by Thomas Kedgwin bare date 1217."

Not a great deal is known of Adams. He notes that he was present at the proclamation of King James I (26 March 1603). Regular entries in his chronicle continue until 1639; the latest event recorded is the execution of Charles I (January 1649), but this may have been added by someone else. A William Adams, perhaps our chronicler, appears in local records as a haberdasher, ironmonger and mercer, and may be identical with one of that name who was apprenticed and admitted to the freedom of Bristol as a draper.[2] Although the chronicle is largely concerned with national history, it also gives illuminating glimpses of incidents in early seventeenth century Bristol, evidently from first-hand knowledge. It shows Adams to have been a churchman and a strong Protestant.

Publication : The chronicle was known only in manuscript until

MS. 2 (see below) was edited, by Miss E. Salisbury, and privately printed for Francis F. Fox, F.S.A. (see No. 44) in 1910, in a limited edition of only 100 copies, as *Adams's Chronicle of Bristol*, unfortunately without any introduction or information on the writer.

MSS. 1. B.R.O., 13748 (4). This seems to be the original manuscript of the chronicle and is more detailed than the version printed from MS. 2. Inside the back cover is written: "Daniel Adams His Book". This Daniel, doubtless a relative, was not William's son if identical with a Danyell Adams, ropemaker, who received his freedom of Bristol as the son of another Danyell.[3] Nineteenth century owners of this MS. included William Tyson, F.S.A. and G.W. Braikenridge, F.S.A.

2. A second manuscript, owned by Samuel Sandys in 1749 and by Joseph Harford (a City Councillor) in the time of the Bristol historian Samuel Seyer (1757 - 1831), was bought after the death of the Rev. F.K. Harford in 1907 by F.F. Fox (see above). It is not in the catalogue of Fox's library, sold in 1930, and has disappeared.

Biographical sources: Bristol Corporation Archives; *TBGAS*, xxxiii, 140-142.

Notes. 1. MS. 1, folio 38.
2. Bristol Corporation: Mayor's Audit, 1600 - 01, p. 138
3. Ibid.: Burgess Register, 14 Feb. 1632/3. This and the previous reference kindly provided by Bristol City Archivist.

5. John THEYER, ?1598 - 1673

The Oxford antiquary Anthony Wood, or à Wood as he latterly styled himself, appears to be the main source of references (e.g. by Ralph Bigland) to John Theyer, and must be a reliable one, since they were personal friends and Wood visited Theyer at Cooper's Hill.[1] According to Wood, Theyer's grandfather Thomas Theyer or Theare married Anne, sister of Richard Hart, the last Prior of Llanthony Secunda near Gloucester; and Thomas Theyer inherited from Prior Hart, whose executor he was, a collection of manuscripts, some of which may have come from the Llanthony library. To these he added substantially and they descended to his grandson John, our antiquary. The latter left a note in Latin, in a manuscript now in the British Library[2]:– "Given to my grandson Charles Theyer, this day, 22 May 1656, by me John Theyer, senior, of Colpers Hill Glos., son of John Theyer, son of Thomas Theyer, late farmer [i.e. the lessee] of the demesne lands of the manor of Brockworth, as appears in the Court of Augmentations." The writer further refers to the date of the MS. (1498) as "102 years before the birth of me, J.T., and 158 years before this day", but the Brockworth parish register records his baptism on the 5th November 1598.

This John Theyer, says Anthony Wood, was

"born of genteel parents at Cooper's Hill in the parish of Brockworth[3], began to be conversant with the Muses in Magdalen College ann. 1611, aet. 16[4] .... gave himself up mostly to the study of venerable antiquity and to the obtaining of .... MSS., in which he did so much abound that no private gentleman of his rank and quality did ever exceed him. He was a lover of learning, a zealous Royalist, ... a bookish and studious man ..."

That Theyer was a Royalist is confirmed by the University archives at Oxford, which record that (having published there in 1643 a religious polemic, *Aerio Mastix*, agreeable to Charles I's High Church views) he was by royal command created Master of Arts, being "then in the King's army". Through the sequestration of his estate by Parliament, when he was described as a 'most inveterate' delinquent, he was greatly impoverished, though not to the extent of parting with his manuscripts. We are told by Wood that he was converted to Catholicism by Queen Henrietta Maria's confessor.

Theyer's reputation was almost exclusively as a collector of manuscripts, said to have numbered 800, but a catalogue probably made in his lifetime gives only 334. They were sold by his grandson Charles (after declining an offer of £100 or more from the Bodleian Library, says Wood) to a London bookseller Robert Scott, who resold them to King Charles II, the last large collection bought for the Royal Manuscripts. They are now in the King's Library (British Library). One MS. given by Charles Theyer to his own college (University College, Oxford) is now in the College library.

Publications : *Aerio Mastix, or a Vindication of the Apostolical and generally received Government of the Church of Christ by Bishops*, 1643. No antiquarian publications are known.

MSS. Anthony Wood says that Theyer wrote 'A friendly Debate between the Protestants and the Papists', but left it unpublished. Two letters from Theyer to Wood, 1663 and 1665, are in Bodl. MS. Wood, D 45. The Bodleian also has (MS Ballard 65) some anonymous historical notes on Gloucestershire, probably of the early 17th century, which include a reference to Brockworth parsonage and may possibly be in Theyer's hand,[5] though there are features of the writing which do not occur in his letters written much later in life. The writer of the notes in question was evidently concerned, amongst other things, with the publication of a map of Gloucestershire, and may have been one of the local antiquaries who are known to have supplied John Speed with information for his county maps.[6]

Biographical sources: D.N.B.; Alumni Oxon.; Anthony à Wood, *Athenae Oxonienses* (1691-2), III, 995-6; *The Life and Times of Anthony Wood,* ed. A. Clark, (Oxf. Hist. Soc.), 1891-1900; *British Library Cat. of Royal & King's MSS*, xxvi; *N. & Q.*, ser. 3, vii, 341, etc.; *Glos. N. & Q.*, 3, 195-6; Rev. S.E. Bartleet, 'The Manor and Advowson of Brockworth', in*TBGAS*, vii, 164-6.

Notes. 1. See Introduction, p. 19.
2. Royal MSS., 6A, viii, f.43.
3. Cooper's Hill is now chiefly known for the annual 'cheese-rolling' which takes place there.
4. The College register says 1613, 'age about 16'. He took no degree then, but proceeded to study law at New Inn, London.
5. I am obliged to Dr. D.M. Barratt of the Bodleian for suggesting this possibility.
6. See Edward Lynam, *British Maps and Map-makers* (1944), p. 25.

6. Abel WANTNER, ?1639 - 1714

Later and more learned historians who alluded disparagingly to Abel Wantner or Wontner, were not too proud to make use of the information he had painstakingly collected but did not manage to publish. William Nicholson, Bishop of Gloucester 1661-1672, thought that Wantner's "busie medling in things beyond his station" merited discouragement; Richard Furney deemed him "very little qualify'd for this work"; and T.S. Fosbroke's verdict on his collections a century later (quoted by G.W. Counsel) was: "happy it is for his memory that they were never published."

Wantner described himself as a "citizen of Gloucester and inhabitant of Minchinhampton",[1] so was presumably a freeman of the city. His tombstone in St. John's church, Gloucester, on which he was called 'gent.', gave his age as 78 and his year of birth has been said to be 1636, but his baptism, as the son of Abel and Margaret Wantner, is entered in the St. John's register on 15 April, 1639. Abel senior, an innkeeper, was churchwarden of the parish in 1635, and the son became parish clerk of St. John's in later life. When middle-aged, in 1685[2], he issued a printed prospectus inviting subscribers for printing a one-volume history of the City and County of Gloucester, the material for which he said he had been collecting for twelve years. The local gentry and clergy proved unresponsive to the humble parish clerk's appeal, but he worked on, and his draft history is dated 1714, the last year of his life. Acquired by Richard Furney after Wantner's death, it remains in manuscript in the Bodleian Library. His memoranda, also extant there, include a short history of Bristol.

Although he wasted much time on second-hand historical preambles, Wantner is observant and well-informed when he comes to dealing with topography and local history. As Dr. Esther Moir has commented, he came nearer to completing a county history than either Parsons or Furney. When Sir Robert Atkyns's history was published posthumously in 1712, Wantner had only two years to live, and must have felt disappointed. Beyond what can be gleaned from his manuscripts and prospectus, we know nothing of his personality, though he seems to have been a vigorous character with views of his own.

Publications: none, other than his prospectus.

MSS. 1. Bodl. Top. Gloucs. c.2 (S.C. 27827): memoranda, heraldic and miscellaneous, on Gloucestershire; printed prospectuses; and Bristol history (1 vol.). This is largely the material used in compiling no. 2 below.

2. Bodl., Top. Gloucs. c.3 (S.C. 27828): five 'books' in one volume, viz. Books 1 and 2, 'The History .... of the Antient City and Royal Dukedom of Gloucester, from its original to this present time, by Abel Wantner, Citizen of Gloster, 1714'; Book 3. the County; Book 4, The Diocese; Book 5, 'the Honorary part' (the nobility and gentry, with their armorial bearings). These were evidently produced at a variety of dates.

3. According to William D. Macray of the Bodleian Library (writing in *Glos. N. & Q.*, 1, 199), Lot 635 in Peter Le Neve's sale of 1731 is described as 'Arms of the Gentry of Gloucestershire, collected by Abel Wantner, 1683'; Macray adds that this was noted in the Bodleian copy of the sale catalogue as having been bought (for three shillings) by the Suffolk antiquary Thomas Martin of Thetford, but did not occur in Martin's sale catalogue of 1773/4. The MS. in question does not appear to be identical with no. 1 above, and its present whereabouts is unknown.

In Sir Thomas Phillipps's Catalogue, item 13524 is described as 'Abel Wantner's Collections for Gloucestershire. Printed [sic] and interleaved with MS. additions. A Topographical Description of Gloucestershire'. This may have been a copy of the *Topographical Description of Gloucestershire*, by John or Samuel Lewis, printed 1712, with MS. addenda by ?Wantner. The fate of this too is not known.

Biographical sources: *Glos. N. & Q.*, 1, 182-3, 199; Esther Moir, 'Historians of Gloucestershire' in *Gloucestershire Studies* (ed. Finberg), 274-6; Brian S. Smith, Introduction to reprint of Atkyns's *Ancient & Present State of Gloucestershire* (1974); information from Mr Brian Frith.

Notes. 1. He was living in Minchinhampton on 11 March 1679/80, when he was a bondsman for a marriage allegation. (*Gloucestershire Marriage Allegations, 1637-1680*, ed. Brian Frith.)

2. The Bodleian Library has also a revised prospectus of 1686.

7. Richard PARSONS, 1643 - 1711

On his memorial in Gloucester Cathedral it is recorded that Richard Parsons died aged 68 on June the 12th, 1711, so that he must have been born in 1643, as stated in the *D.N.B.*, and not in 1639, the year noted — not by himself — in his Bodleian Library manuscript. In fact it was not until 1641 that his father, the Rev. Dr. William Parsons (later a Canon of Chichester) became Rector of Birchanger, Essex, where Richard was born. At Winchester he was entered as 'founder's kin', and he became a Fellow of New College, Oxford. Having in 1674 been presented to the living of Driffield, Gloucestershire, and three years later[1] appointed to the Chancellorship of the Gloucester Diocese, he held both preferments for the rest of his life. According to his memorial he was "diligent in the execution of his office, and eminent as well for hospitality to strangers as charity to the poor." In 1687 he became, like his father, a Doctor of Civil Law.

In his business excursions through the diocese, visiting every church, the Chancellor compiled the large and interesting volume of notes now in the Bodleian, and, it seems, a second volume long since lost. The idea of attempting to write a county history is said to have been suggested to him by Henry Wharton (1664 - 1695), Archbishop Sancroft's chaplain. Parsons, however, does not appear to have made any serious attempt to weld his notes into a book, and as Sir Robert Atkyns tells us in the preface to his own Gloucestershire history, "indisposition of health prevented his good intentions." His labours were not altogether wasted, as he evidently allowed Atkyns, who died in the same year as Parsons but was four years younger, to make use of his collections. Mr Brian Smith, in his Introduction to the 1974 reprint of Atkyns's *Ancient and Present State of Glostershire*, describes the Parsons manuscript and analyses Atkyns's discriminating borrowings from Parsons.[2]

Publications: none.

MSS. Bodl., MS. Rawlinson B.323 (S.C. 11662), 'A Parochial Visitation of the County of Gloucester'. John Nichols, in *Literary Anecdotes*, ix, 425-7, quotes a letter of 1765 from A.C. Ducarel to Bishop Warburton of Gloucester, saying that the Parsons MS. went first to the Rev. Jonathan Colby, then to Peter Le Neve, at whose sale (1730) it fetched £3:16:0. Thomas Martin of Palgrave, the Suffolk topographer, told Ducarel that it might have been sold to Rawlinson. It came to the Bodleian in 1755 with the rest of the Rawlinson MSS.

Biographical sources: *D.N.B.*; *Athenae Oxonienses* (1721), II, 990; John Nichols, *Literary Anecdotes*, ix, 425-7, 625-6; *N. & Q.*, ser. 6, v, 347, 394; Brian S. Smith, *Introduction* to reprint of Atkyns's *Ancient & Present State of Glostershire* (1974), p. ix.

Notes. 1. i.e. 1677, not 1669, as wrongly stated in the *Alumni Oxonienses*.
2. "He made .... collections towards the history and antiquities of Gloster, of which some tho' little use was made", says the *Athenae Oxon.*, rather unfairly, "in that pompous but injudicious piece published by Sir Robert Atkyns."

8. Sir Robert ATKYNS, 1647 - 1711

Sir Robert Atkyns the younger, author of Gloucestershire's first printed county history, was baptised at Monken Hadley, Herts.[1] on 26 August 1647. He came of a Gloucestershire legal family of some distinction, for his grandfather, Sir Edward Atkyns, was a judge both under the Commonwealth and after the Restoration, and his father, Sir Robert (1620 - 1709/10) became Chief Baron of the Exchequer and Speaker of the House of Lords. Robert Atkyns junior, who had been at St. Edmund Hall, Oxon., was called to the bar in the family tradition. Thanks to parental influence, he was knighted in 1663 at the age of sixteen, made an F.R.S. at seventeen, and from 1673 to 1679 held the office of Comptroller of Law Duties, probably a sinecure. He became a J.P. for Gloucestershire in 1673, a Deputy Lieutenant in 1683, M.P. for Cirencester 1679-81 and for the County 1685 - 87, but he seems to have been overshadowed by his father — who died aged 88 only two years before the son — and they disagreed over politics. Whereas Sir Robert the elder achieved high office by becoming a Whig under William III, his son refused to take the oath of allegiance to William and remained a Tory. So did his uncle Sir Edward Atkyns, junior, another judge, who consequently resigned the office of Chief Baron, in which his brother succeeded him in 1689.

Thus Sir Robert the younger retired into country life and historical research in Gloucestershire. The family seat had been at Tuffley near Gloucester, but his father had bought the manors of Nether Swell in 1659, Sapperton in 1660, and Pinbury Park (in Duntisbourne Rous) in 1661. The son lived at Pinbury in later life. Little can be discerned about his personality or local activities, though we have his portrait, engraved by Michael Van der Gucht, as the frontispiece to the *Ancient and Present State of Glostershire* (1st edn.).

Considerable efforts have failed to trace a single letter, note, or document in Atkyns's handwriting, though a man in his position must surely have had many correspondents. There is, however, the copy of a letter from Atkyns to the antiquary Browne Willis (1682 - 1760), unfortunately not dated, which tells us something of his rather hesitating project. It was written from Pinbury Park on April 11, (no year),[2] and is now B.L. Add. 5841, p.43.

I received your letter and the inclosed papers with great satisfaction: it gave me a new incouragement to proceed in the intended History of Glocestershire. I have hitherto had no assistance, & I was truly sensible of my own unfitnesse for such an undertaking. I therefore beg the continuance of your favour & that you would send as many books & papers as you please to Mrs. Beake at the Cabinet against Turnstile in Holborn, & she will take care to convey them safe to me.

I very much covet a further acquaintance with you; but I know not how to hope for it before winter at London: unlesse you had thoughts of coming to Somerford or to Bath or to Bristol sometime this summer. But if your good nature shall induce you to come to Pinbury Parke, I shall then think myselfe extreamly happy, & I can assure you of a most hearty welcome to [sic]

Your most obliged humble servant
Ro. Atkyns

Mr. Brydges presents his service to you & importunately joynes with me to invite you hither.

"Mr. Brydges" must be his niece Annabella's husband the Hon. & Rev. Henry Brydges, D.D., a son of the 8th Lord Chandos, who was Rector of Broadwell with Adlestrop, Glos., 1699 - 1717, and Archdeacon of Rochester from 1720 until his death in 1728. The postscript suggests that Henry Brydges may have helped in his uncle's researches and perhaps also may have seen his history through the press after his death. If not, who did?

Atkyns, in his preface, says: "The present work is published by a lay hand, whose true and hearty love for his country excited him to this performance .... It had been more advisable to have ended this account about fifty or sixty years since, and not to have carried it on to this present time; for when there is a necessity to depend upon message - informations we must then expect many mistakes." These message - informations, presumably, were reports on current or recent events in the county, obtained by proxy. Atkyns's own work, other than editorial, seems to have been largely confined to the examination of historical records; he was indebted also, as he acknowledges, to the collections made by the Rev. Richard Parsons.[3] As a recent commentator observes, "he was not the sort of antiquarian to ride around the countryside inspecting churches and measuring earthworks, deciphering inscriptions or recording local legends."[4] He showed, however, a rather modern interest in population statistics.

When Sir Robert Atkyns died in 1711 his history was still unpublished, but it appeared in 1712, as *The Ancient and Present*

State of Glostershire. The monument erected by his widow in Sapperton church claims, not without justice, that "he left behind him one more durable" in his county history. He has a later memorial tablet in Ketteringham church, Norfolk. There is a pedigree of the family in *TBGAS*, vol. 50, facing page 236.

Publication: *The Ancient and Present State of Glostershire*, 1712 (2nd edn., unrevised, 1768. Reissued 1974, with Introduction by Brian S. Smith, F.S.A.). Atkyns wrote nothing else.

MSS. Nothing in Atkyns's autograph has been found, except for some signatures on deeds. The transcriber of his letter to Browne Willis (see above) notes that it was in 'a neat Italic hand'. Confusion with his father, many of whose letters survive, is easy. A letter signed Robert Atkyns to the Bishop of Oxford (Bodl. Libr. MS. Rawl. D 399, f. 279), graphically describing the ruinous state of Lower Swell church and its want of a good incumbent[5], is evidently from Sir Robert Atkyns, senior, and so, no doubt, was a letter to 'Mr. Lysons' of which 'E.C.S.' (Sewell) gives a copy in *Glos. N. & Q.*, 3, 513, as it refers to the writer's grandson.

Much of the first edition of the *Ancient & Present State of Glostershire* was destroyed by fire, 29 Jan. 1712/13, at the printer's house in London. The statement, in *N. & Q.*, ser. 2, xi, 201, that the original MS. of a second volume also perished, comes from an MS. entitled *Adversaria*, by William Oldys, herald and antiquary, and is probably untrue. If any manuscript was destroyed, it was doubtless that of the existing volume, which is complete in itself and contains no suggestion that another was contemplated, let alone completed.

Sir Robert, junior, had no children. His chief heir was a nephew, Robert, who left two daughters. In 1753 most of the Atkyns property went to a cousin, Edward Atkyns of Ketteringham Hall, Norfolk, where the family died out in the early 19th century. J.D. Thorp's lengthy paper (see below) yields much information on the family and the descent of the estate, but if the historian left any notes or other papers they have most likely not survived.

Biographical sources: *D.N.B.*; *Man. G. Lit.*, I, 14 - 19; Roland Austin, 'Some Account of Sir Robert Atkyns the younger and other members of the Atkyns family', in *TBGAS*, xxxv; J.D. Thorp, 'A History of the Manor of Coates', in *TBGAS*, l; Brian S. Smith, Introduction to reprint of *The Ancient & Present State of Glostershire*, 1974; *Glos. N. & Q.*, 1, 334-5.

Notes.
1. The *D.N.B.* says, in error, that he was born in Gloucestershire. Austin (*loc. cit. infra*) corrects the dates of his birth and death.
2. The letter is addressed to *Richard* Willis, but is among correspondence of Browne Willis copied by the Cambridge antiquary William Cole, so 'Richard' is doubtless a mistake by Atkyns, who had apparently made some slight acquaintance with Willis in London. Willis must then have been quite young, but he was a Member of Parliament at 23, and they may have met at Westminster.
3. See No. 7.
4. Brian S. Smith, see *Biographical sources*.
5. Printed, with commentary, by C.R. Elrington, F.S.A., in *TBGAS*, lxxxi.

9. John PRINN or PRYNNE, 1661 or 1662 - 1735

According to Ralph Bigland, John Prinn (thus he spelt it himself) was said to have been a 'collateral descendant' of William Prynne (1600 - 1669), the Puritan lawyer, agitator and pamphleteer who lost his ears for *lese-majesté* under Charles I and later fell foul of Cromwell, but became Keeper of the public records in the Tower of London under Charles II.[1]

John, likewise a lawyer and interested in records, was admitted to Clifford's Inn in 1681, migrated to the Inner Temple in 1684, and was called to the Bar in 1689. The Clifford's Inn registers are not extant, and the Inner Temple admission register does not give his parentage or birthplace. He was described as "gent., of Reading, Berks.", when his son John matriculated at Oxford in 1702,[2] but his residence there may have been temporary, as the Berkshire Record Office has been unable to trace him. He later had a wide legal practice in north Gloucestershire and was for many years steward of the important manor of Cheltenham. In 1697 he bought the manor of Ashley and the Charlton Park estate in Charlton Kings, adjacent to Cheltenham, where his descendants lived until the 19th century.

Most of our information about Prinn's antiquarian tastes is derived from a long footnote, under Charlton Kings, in Bigland's History of Gloucestershire. This states that

> "About the year 1737[3] John Prynne esq. completed his MSS. and prepared them for the Press; a design which has never been completed. They consist of collections chiefly emendatory of Sir R. Atkyns's History .... besides many interesting and curious additions. Mr. Prynne pursued his laborious investigations with that unwearied industry and arrangement by which alone correctness can be acquired ...".

On February the 9th, 1732, however, Prinn had written to George Ballard[4] (No. 12):–

> "Tis not my design to appear in print. The book you mention may be improv'd, — and I shall be willing to put a helping hand to it .... monuments and inscriptions in churches are beside my purpose ...."
> "P.S. I want a book entitled *Chartae Antiquae* & can't meet with it."

'The book you mention' is presumably Atkyns's history. At all events it is clear that Prinn, like Atkyns himself, was addicted to documentary research more than to topography or local monuments. Nor, apparently, did he have publication seriously in view in 1732, only three years before his death.

T.D. Fosbroke says that Prinn extracted or rather copied the contents of the Registers [cartularies] of Gloucester, Cirencester and Winchcombe Abbeys, papers of Gloucester Corporation, Dean & Chapter, and other records. He is also said to have 'preserved' the Cirencester cartulary.

The usually reliable A.N.L. Munby gave Prinn's dates incorrectly as 1686 - 1743. His memorial at Charlton Kings says that he died on 26 Feb. 1734 [i.e. 1734/5], aged 73. The *Gentleman's Magazine* and *Musgrave's Obituary* have the date of death as 6 Mar. 1735. John Prinn's will (P.C.C. Prob. 11/670), made in 1716 and proved 20 Mar. 1734/5 by his son the Rev. John Prinn, gives a glimpse of his character and domestic life. (He had married a widow). Apart from small bequests, he left his whole estate to his son, describing himself as "father of John Prinn, a son most dutyfull, and Ann Prinn, a daughter most undutyfull of children". To his "worthless daughter", aged 28 in 1716, who had "chosen to rely upon the charity of well disposed persons ('tis her own expression) rather than to accept of £1,100 of mine and marry the best deserving man in Europe", he gave "not more than a corn of pepper, to be paid her by my executor [her brother] if she demands it."

It is also worthy of mention that Prinn took up to the House of Lords, and lost, a lawsuit brought against him for slander by John Grubham Howe (Jack Howe, the political turncoat and County member) who alleged that Prinn, in Cirencester market, had said: "Do not vote for Howe, he is a Jacobite and is for bringing in the Prince of Wales [the Old Pretender] and Popery, to destroy our nation."[5]

Publications: apparently none. Prinn's abbreviated *Winchcombe Cartulary* (Glos. Coll. 11788) was lithographed by Sir Thomas Phillips at the Middle Hill Press, from a 19th century copy.

MSS. 1. What was the fate of Prinn's "collections"? Bigland (*loc. cit. supra*) thanked "Dodington Hunt, the present possessor" for letting him make use of them. Hunt, married to Elizabeth, heiress of John Prinn's grandson William, had inherited the Charlton Park estate and Prinn's papers.

The next we hear of these papers, or some of them, is in the famous catalogue of Sir Thomas Phillipps (No. 32), as nos. 7873 - 80, described as 'Prinn MSS.: 7873, collections and memoranda; 7874, Arms of gentry in England and precedents of legal deeds; 7875, Glos. County Poll Book, 1734; 7876, Cheltenham Poll Book, 17..; 7877, Essays and Prize Poems at .... School, c. 1730; 7878, Extracts from Winchcombe Cartulary; 7879 (folio vol of 592 pp.), Collections for Gloucestershire; 7880, memoranda out of Cirencester Register [cartulary]. Phillipps notes against these items '*Donum amici*' and the link is completed by no. 7878, which is now Bodl. MS. Phillipps-Robinson c. 131. On this Phillipps has noted: 'MSS. of Captain Prowse, Charlton Park.' Clearly the 'amicus' was George Bragge Prowse, upon whom the Charlton estate had devolved in 1821 on the death of William Hunt Prynne, Dodington Hunt's son. W.H. Hunt had taken the name of Prynne, and Prowse also assumed this name and arms in 1825.

Of the other Phillipps items, 7874 is at the Univ. of Michigan, U.S.A., and 7875 is in the Gloucester Library. The present whereabouts of the rest is unknown, but their description gives a fair idea of Prinn's interests.

2. In Registers A and B of St. Peter's Abbey, Gloucester (now in Gloucester Cathedral Library) there are indexes and annotations in Prinn's distinctive handwriting. He was also responsible for MS. 35 in the Cathedral Library, a collection of transcripts relating to the Bishops and Deans & Chapters, with some notes on the City of Gloucester.[6]

3. In the Cheltenham Manor court books (G.R.O., D 855 M), Prinn,(the steward of the manor) has inserted some local history of Cheltenham. Some of the court books are annotated as having been missing and retrieved by Prinn.

4. Records of the Charlton Park estate were in 1952 in the possession of a descendant, Lady Magnus-Allcroft, at Stokesay Court, Salop. These include a MS. catalogue of the Library of John Prinn's grandson, with other Prinn family records, but apparently no antiquarian MSS. (List in G.R.O.)

Biographical sources: R. Bigland, *Hist. of Gloucestershire*, I, 299; *N. & Q.*, ser. 5, viii, 207, 279, 517, and ser. 9, ii, 288, 336; *Norman's Hist. of Cheltenham*, 1863 edn., 94 - 102; Gwen Hart, *Hist. of Cheltenham* (1965), 122 - 3.

Notes.
1. The relationship is obscure, and is not mentioned by R.E.M. Peach in his *Annals of the Parish of Swanswick*, Somerset (1890), where he deals with William Prynne's family in some detail. John Prinn, perhaps a cousin, could have been the son of another William Prynne, gent., whose epitaph in Cheltenham Parish Church is given by a correspondent 'A.B.H.' in *N. & Q.*, 15 Sept. 1877, p. 207.
2. *Alumni Oxon.* He was M.A. from Oriel, 1708, Rector of Shipton Oliffe and Shipton Sollers, Glos., from 1711. 'The Rev. Mr. Prinn' was buried at Charlton Kings, 1743, aged 57.
3. This is of course wrong, since Prinn died in 1735, but Bigland's known connection with Gloucestershire starts with his marriage in 1737, so they probably never met.
4. Bodl., Ballard 40 (S.C. 10826), fol. 132.
5. The B.L. has a copy of *Mr. Prinn's Answer to Mr. Howe's Printed Case*.
6. See Isabel Kirby, *Diocese of Gloucester* (Archives), 1967 - 8, Vol. II, pp. 1 and 25.

10. Richard GRAVES, 1677 - 1729

Of some antiquaries nothing survives either in print or in manuscript, and of such is Richard Graves, senior, the squire of Mickleton near Chipping Campden. Yet we have it on good authority that he made large collections of historical material for the Gloucestershire Hundred of Kiftsgate, and intended to publish a history of the Vale of Evesham.

The Graves pedigree and a portrait of Richard Graves are to be found in Nash's *History of Worcestershire*.[1] Richard, the eldest son of Samuel Graves of Mickleton Manor, was at Chipping Campden Grammar School under a notable headmaster, Robert Morse. In 1693 he proceeded to Pembroke College, Oxford, and in the same year was entered at Lincoln's Inn. Our best account of him has been given by George Ballard (No. 12), who seems to have owed to Graves his introduction to Oxford and the intellectual world.

> "Being delighted with a private life, he retired to his Manor House at Mickleton, where he chiefly spent the remaining part of his life in the study of antiquities. He was a very obliging communicative gentleman .... admirably well read .... and a most curious historian, antiquary, and medallist."[2]

Thomas Hearne told Ballard that Graves

> "had just before his death finish'd collecting what he thought would be of service to his performance, & had 3 folio volumes of blank paper neatly bound up, in order to have digested and compleated his designs, but was untimely prevented by death."[3]

Richard Graves was only fifty-one when he died. A number of his letters to Thomas Hearne of Oxford, from 1715 to 1725, are in the Bodleian Library.[4] He was also, he tells Hearne, nearly related to Dr. Samuel Knight (1675 - 1746), historical biographer and founder-member of the Society of Antiquaries. There is a monument with a long Latin panegyric, in Mickleton church. His son, the Rev. Richard Graves, was the author of *The Spiritual Quixote* — a satire on Whitefield and the Methodists and a best-seller in its day — and other novels.

Publications: none.

MSS. Richard Graves's collections of manuscripts, according to

Ballard, were bought by Graves's friend James West, P.R.S. (see *D.N.B.*) and after West's death by the Earl of Shelburne (afterwards 1st Marquess of Lansdowne). They do not appear to be among the Lansdowne papers, but perhaps some of them may turn up eventually. Hearne observed :– "I don't know whether Mr. West purchased all his papers, for his son Morgan Graves Esq, being in no way curious in these matters, might mislay and carelessly make away with some of those valuable papers."[3]
In the late 19th century there was still at Mickleton Manor one volume, badly damaged by fire, containing MS. notes on the Graves family and Mickleton.[5] In 1955 Miss Graves-Hamilton of St. Albans had family portraits and some papers (see N.R.A. Report 6455), but no literary or antiquarian MSS. except a map of Mickleton manor by Richard Graves.

Biographical sources: *D.N.B*; *Glos. N. & Q.*, 1, 221 and 3, 480; Sir John Maclean, 'The Family of Graves', in *The Genealogist*, iv, 103 -06; Nichols, *Literary Anecdotes*, ii, 467 - 9.

Notes:
1. Vol. I, 198 - 9.
2. Ballard, letter to Richard Rawlinson, Bodl., MSS. Rawl. J.3/177 (S.C. 15508).
3. Hearne to Ballard, quoted in Bodl., MSS. Rawl. J.3/94 (S.C. 15508).
4. Rawl. lett. 15/41 - 50 (S.C. 15578)
5. *D.N.B.* (inf. from Sidney Graves-Hamilton).

11. Richard FURNEY, 1694 - 1753

Like Richard Parsons a generation or so earlier, Archdeacon Furney left a substantial amount of manuscript and later historians have profited from his labours, but he published nothing.

He was christened at St. Michael's, Gloucester, on 12 June 1694, as the son of James Furney,[1] who is described as 'gent.' in Richard's admission to Oriel, Oxon. in February 1711/12; this is doubtless the James Furney who was City Sheriff of Gloucester in 1698 and Mayor in 1710. The son became Rector of Doynton, near Bristol, in 1720, but presumably put in a curate for his distant parish, for he was also Master of the Crypt Grammar School in Gloucester from about 1720 to 1724.

It was in 1720 that the City Council of Gloucester devised a 'Scheme for the regulating and putting in order the records, books and writings belonging to the City', which resulted in the compilation of a large folio catalogue in manuscript, now GBR 1704 in the City Archives. From recent research by Mrs. Margaret Richards of the Gloucestershire Record Office, it is evident that Richard Furney was responsible for arranging or 'methodising' the records.[2] In August 1720 we find him writing to the Oxford scholar Thomas Hearne (1678 - 1735): " .... I am now very warmly engaged in looking over vast quantities of records". Letters of Furney's to Hearne, dated between 1720 and 1729[3], show him to have been a serious and dedicated student and book-collector, and he certainly contemplated attempting a county history.

His removal from the West Country may explain why he never carried out his intentions. In August 1724 he told Hearne that he was still Rector of Doynton, but that the Bishop of Winchester had made him one of his chaplains. From 1727 he was Rector of Houghton, and from 1729 of Cheriton, both in Hampshire, and in 1725, at the age of 31, he had become Archdeacon of Surrey.

Little more is heard of Furney as an antiquary, but in his later years part at least of his time was spent at Hucclecote, near Gloucester, whence he wrote on 25 January 1743/4 to Browne Willis, the antiquary (1682 - 1760). A copy of a manuscript compilation by Furney concerning Gloucester city is dated 1749 (see below, MSS. 1). He died at Hucclecote in February 1753, aged 58, and was buried at St. Michael's, Gloucester, where he had been baptised. In the church, of which only the tower now remains, there was a brief memorial.[4] To the Bodleian Library he bequeathed six manuscript volumes (see below). His name is not in the *Dictionary of National Biography*, but Thomas Hearne refers to him as "my learned friend" and he assisted Hearne in his publication of Peter Langtoft's Chronicle (1725), in which two of Furney's letters are printed (pp. 68 and 201 - 06). Browne Willis wrote of him in 1758 to his fellow-antiquary Andrew Coltée Ducarel (1713 - 85): "He was a great acquaintance and correspondent of mine, and I was very instrumental in his studying venerable antiquity."[5]

Publications: none.

MSS. 1. Bodl., MSS. Top. Gloucs., 4 vols. viz. b.1 (S.C. 27825), copies of Glos. Inquisitions Post Mortem; c.1 (S.C. 27826), Gloucester city transcripts, etc.; c. 4 and 5, 'The City and Suburbs of Gloucester', apparently a copy by a clerk with some corrections by the author, but Furney's name is not mentioned. c. 4 is dated 1749. The other two volumes of Furney's bequest were MSS of Abel Wantner of Gloucester (see No. 6).

2. Bodl., MSS. Top. Gloucs., e.1 (S.C. 29757), bought at auction at Messrs. Bruton Knowles of Gloucester, April 1887. 'E libris Richard Furney'. Descriptions of personal visits to buildings in Gloucester and neighbourhood, information from named informants, and copies of memorial inscriptions. (Small vol.)

3. G.R.O., D. 327.Notes on history of Gloucester city (1 vol.) This came to the Record Office from Sir Francis Hyett (No. 46). In it is a note by B(enjamin) H(yett), 1807 :"This MS. history of Gloucester was purchased on the decease of the Rev. Samuel Rogers, Canon of St. Davids, and was compiled by the Rev. — Furney, Archdeacon of Surrey, and seems to have been intended for publication." A writer in *N. & Q.*, ser. 1, xi, 205, says that Furney's collections for the city passed to the Rev. Richard Rogers, incumbent of St. Mary de Crypt, Gloucester. Samuel Rudder (preface to his county history, 1779) says: "The history of the City and Diocese is newly drawn up from materials collected by the late Revd. Mr. Furney, and communicated to Mr. Rogers of Gloucester", which might refer either to the volume in the G.R.O. (above) or to the 'collections' (see below) now in the Gloucester Library. But T.D. Fosbroke, in the preface to his Gloucester City history of 1819, remarks that Furney made only a 'catalogue raisonné', not a history, containing only 126 folio pages.

4. Glos. Coll. 3281. 'Collections relating to the City and Diocese' (4 vols.), viz. 'A.' Notes and transcripts of documents belonging to the Dean & Chapter of Gloucester; 'B.' 'Collections from original records, deeds etc., in the office of the Bishop's Register [Registrar] and the Treasury of the City of Gloucester,' made in 1721; 'C.' a catalogue, by city streets and rural parishes, of records in the Gloucester Diocesan Registry and City Corporation Archives; 'D.' Biblical commentaries etc., appears to have no connection with Furney.

Volumes A and C were presented to the Bristol & Gloucestershire Archaeological Society in 1899 by John Norton, an architect, of London, who (in a letter inserted in Vol. A) wrote: "I am unable to trace the history of its possession, except that it has been in my family, I believe, the greater part of a century." Volume B had been bought by the Society "at Lysons sale, April 1887".

5. Phillipps MSS. 6632 - 38 (7 vols.), sold at Sotheby's on 28 June 1965, are now MS. Add. 400 in the Folger Shakespeare Library, Washington, U.S.A. (photocopy in B.L., R.P. 2, 6 (1)). These must be the seven volumes stated by Sir Thomas Phillipps in his catalogue, 1837, p. 98, to have been acquired from G.W. Counsel of Gloucester. For an exchange of letters about this sale, see illustrations 18 and 32 in the present book. On the fly-leaves of Vol. 1 Counsel wrote an account of Furney and the history of his manuscripts. The contents are mainly extracts from Gloucestershire records including monastic cartularies, but Vol. 7 relates to the Winchester diocese.

Biographical sources: *Alumni Oxon.* ; *N. & Q.*, ser. 1, xi, 205 and xii, 95, 387-8; *Glos. N. & Q.*, 1, 384-7 and 2, 390; Macray, *Annals of the Bodleian Library,* 184; Thos. Hearne, *Collections* (Oxf. Hist. Soc.), vols. 6 - 10; Bodl., MS. Rawlinson, v, 262.

Notes:
1. Mr. Brian Frith has kindly obtained the parish register entry.
2. Mrs. Richardson has found evidence suggesting that Volume 'C', under *MSS* 4, above, is Furney's draft of the inventory of City records, GBR 1704, mentioned in the preceding sentence.
3. Bodl., Rawl. lett. 5, 230 *et seq.* (29 letters)
4. Copy in *N. & Q.*, ser. 1, xii, 387-8.
5. *N. & Q.*, *loc. cit.*

12. George BALLARD, 1706 - 1755

Born at Chipping Campden, George Ballard was a great-nephew of John Ballard (1612 - 78), who was a physician and a contributor to the *Annalia Dubrensia*.[1] The family must have come down in the world, for George is described as a stay-maker's apprentice, but he spent his spare time in gathering local history, collecting coins, and studying Anglo-Saxon. Introduced by Richard Graves of Mickleton (No. 10) to the Oxford antiquary Thomas Hearne (1678 - 1735), he became from 1726 a protégé and correspondent of Hearne. A letter from Graves to Hearne, 3 Mar. 1729/30, refers to the large coin collection of Ballard, "who tells me he has travell'd above 1500 miles (most part on foot) in searching after 'em".[2] The young man had also made the acquaintance of Elizabeth Elstob of Evesham, the Anglo-Saxon scholar (see *D.N.B.*).

Eventually, with an annuity of £60 provided by some local gentlemen, including Lord Chedworth, who were impressed with his capabilities, Ballard moved to Oxford, becoming a clerk at Magdalen and later one of the University Bedells. He helped Joseph Ames (1689 - 1759) with his work on the history of printing, and somehow acquired the valuable letters and papers of Dr. Arthur Charlett, Master of University College (1655 - 1722) and of Thomas Rawlins of Pophill. By his will of 1754 (he died, it was reported, from overwork) George Ballard left to the Bodleian Library 72 or 73 manuscripts, including 44 volumes of letters, of which five volumes are addressed to himself.

Publications: none, except for a work entitled *British Ladies .... celebrated for their Writings*.

MSS. 1. Bodleian Libr., MSS. Ballard Colln. (see above - mainly not his own writings)
    2. Chipping Campden Parish Church Museum: Notes for a history of Campden, 1731.

Biographical sources: *D.N.B.*; John Nichols, *Literary Anecdotes of the 18th Century*, 1812 - 16, vol. 2, 466 - 70 and vol. 4, 112 - 40; Bodl. *Introduction to MSS. Ballard Collection*; Esther Moir, 'Historians of Gloucestershire', in *Gloucestershire Studies* (ed. H.P.R. Finberg), 1957.

Notes. 1. See Chr. Whitfield, *Robert Dover and the Cotswold Games*, 1962, p.153.
2. Bodl., Rawl. lett. 6 (S.C. 15572). See also Introduction, p.21.

13. Ralph BIGLAND, 1711 - 1784

This member of an old Lancashire family, who became a Gloucestershire county historian, was born at Stepney and apprenticed to a London cheesemonger; it was perhaps in search of Dutch cheeses that he travelled in the Low Countries when young. He is first recorded in Gloucestershire in 1737, when he married Ann Wilkins of Frocester, near Stroud. Twenty years later, having cultivated uncommercial hobbies while earning his living,[1] he entered the College of Arms, at the age of 46, as Bluemantle Pursuivant, rising in course of time to Somerset Herald, Norroy, Clarencieux, and in 1780 Garter Principal King of Arms. Besides being a keen herald and genealogist, he was an artist of some ability.

Bigland, who had installed his son Richard as lessee of Frocester Court, devoted much of his time in later life to collecting material for a history of the county. Despite its high-sounding title, the eventual book is very sketchy and based on little documentary research. Its author was in fact more of an antiquary than an historian, and the great value of his work lies in the mass of monumental inscriptions — many now illegible or destroyed in 19th century 'restoration' — which he and an unknown number of helpers copied throughout the county. Genealogies were to have formed a separate section of the history, but they never appeared, and are part of Bigland's collections now in the College of Arms.

Like Atkyns, Ralph Bigland died leaving his book unpublished. Before his death in 1784 he had assembled most of the material and arranged much of it, written the preface, and apparently prepared part of the work for the press. Volume I (127 parishes) was issued by his son Richard in 1791, and Volume II (53 parishes) in parts, between 1786 and 1794, under the editorship of James Dallaway.[2] This took the alphabetical series of parishes as far as Newent. The 'Bigland Continuations', completing the work, were printed piecemeal in nine parts, from 1838 onwards, by the bibliophil Sir Thomas Phillipps and his executors.[3] Some instalments were in very limited editions, so that complete copies are to-day exceedingly scarce. The unpublished drafts for Gloucester City had been used by T.D. Fosbroke in his *History of Gloucester*, 1819.[4]

Bigland's portrait as Somerset Herald, by Richard Brompton, in the College of Arms, is reproduced as Plate III in *TBGAS* lxxv. There is a tablet to his memory in the nave of Gloucester Cathedral. The historian is to be distinguished from his nephew Ralph Bigland junior (1757 - 1838), who also became Garter King of Arms and was knighted in 1821, but was otherwise a mediocrity.

Publications: *Observations on Marriages, Baptisms and Burials, as preserved in Parochial Registers*, 1764; *Historical, Monumental & Genealogical Collections relative to the County of Gloucester*, 1791 onwards, as described above.

MSS. 1. After the custom of Heralds, Bigland bequeathed his heraldic and genealogical collections to the College of Arms.

2. The story of Bigland's Gloucestershire 'collections' can be to some extent traced. Fosbroke (*History of Gloucester*, preface) tells us that "the epitaphs collected by Mr. Bigland form a MS. octavo volume, in a neat small hand, written on both sides, *four inches thick*" (Fosbroke's italics). A contributor to *Glos. N. & Q.*, 1, 111, writes: "After the publication of Vols. I and II, the MSS. probably remained with Messrs. Nichols, the printers, who issued proposals for continuing publication by subscription, with T.D. Fosbroke as editor. The MSS., chiefly undigested notes, then passed to Sir Thomas Phillipps by purchase." For Phillipps's publication of Bigland's 'Continuations', see above.

3. Phillipps catalogues numerous items as 'Bigland's', but several of these, though Bigland may have owned them, are other people's manuscripts. The history of about a dozen others is not known; they may be part of the final residue of the Phillipps Collection acquired by M.P. Kraus of New York. Of the remainder, 10563 (Oxfordshire) was sold at Sotheby's on 10 June 1896. 10572 (Glos. church notes, N - Z, a large bundle), 13519[5] (Bigland's original note-books for his History, bks. 3,6,7,9,10), 18113 (collections for Glos.), and 21025 (Glos., letter N. and some other parishes, and cathedral) were sold at Sotheby's, 26 June 1967. Perhaps also 10571, if identical with the two quarto vols., in one hand, with interpolations by Phillipps and others, which were offered by Stanley Crowe, the London antiquarian bookseller, in 1973 (his cat. no. 83); the purchaser has not been traced. 10573 (not traced) may be the vol. described by Fosbroke (para. 2, above). 11194 (genealogical and heraldic) appeared as item 266 in Quaritch's catalogue 987 of 1978. 10574 (epitaphs in Swindon, Wilts.), 14270 (Glos. clergy), 16742 (Gloucr. Cathedral), 21656

(collections for Gloucester) and 22202 (pedigrees) are all now in the Phillipps-Robinson MSS. in the Bodleian Library, which also has 14265-6, sold by Stanley Crowe (his cat. 89). 15336 (not all by Bigland) and 20673 (armorial) were sold at Sotheby's on 6 June 1898 and 15639 (ancient words) on 26 June 1974. 21442 is in the Glos. Coll. (131 later parishes in the alphabetical series, used for the Bigland Continuations).

4. Glos. Coll. 12401 is a group of papers and letters of the Bigland family, 1726 - 1812, some in Ralph Bigland senior's hand, chiefly relating to business and legal matters.

Biographical sources: *D.N.B.*; Mark Noble, *History of the College of Arms*, 1805; Hyett and Austin, *Bibl. Man. of Glos. Lit.*; Irvine Gray, 'Ralph Bigland and his family', in *TBGAS*, lxxv, 116 - 133.

Notes. 1. In his book on parish registers, he quotes monumental inscriptions copied during his "residence in Flanders, Holland, etc.", and others from Edinburgh and Leith.
2. See p. 87.
3. For the full story, see the *Man. Glos. Lit.*
4. See p. 82.
5. 13519 came to Phillipps from the Smith-Pigott library at Brockley Hall, Somerset, sold in 1849.

14. Samuel RUDDER, 1726 - 1801

Not every antiquary of the eighteenth century was a parson or a country squire. Roger Rutter, an eccentric vegetarian of respectable but fairly humble status, lived at Stoutshill in Uley, where his only child Samuel was born.[1] The family changed their name to Rudder about 1748.[2] Samuel, having no doubt shown literary leanings, was apprenticed to a printer, and before 1752 had set up a printing press of his own in Cirencester, where he was already established as a bookseller. He is also described in 1757 as a "dealer in cheese, bacon and salt butter."[3] Samuel Rudder was constable of Cirencester c. 1758, attended vestry meetings, and sat on juries. The first books he printed were Busby's Latin Grammar and a spelling book.

Rudder himself records, in the memoranda on his proof sheets (see *MSS* 1 below) that while still at Uley he "collected his first ideas for a county history". Later Lord Bathurst, the Cirencester magnate, afterwards the first Earl, counselled him to revise Atkyns's history rather than attempt a new one. Rudder issued proposals for publication in February 1767, but was disconcerted by the appearance of the second (unrevised) edition of Atkyns in 1768, and hastily published his *History of the Parish and Abbey of Hayles*, 'proposed as a specimen of a new history of the county'. In December 1771 a notice in the *Gloucester Journal* gave reasons for delays, but the book was still on the stocks five years later, and in December 1776 the author had to reply in the St. James's Chronicle to a request from impatient subscribers for an explanation. The *New History of Gloucestershire* at last emerged in 1779.[4] It was, on the whole, well received; and it is certainly enlivened by Rudder's comments on local conditions and affairs, derived from personal knowledge,[5] whereas Atkyns had relied mainly on documentary and second-hand information. Rudder's references to contemporary archaeological finds are also of value. Considering the writer's lack of academic learning, and the busy life he led, it is a remarkable achievement. The *D.N.B.* quotes Horace Walpole (Letters, vii, 299) as writing that Rudder's "additions to Sir R. Atkyns make it the most sensible history of a county we have had yet".

In his preface Rudder acknowledges that "the history of the City and Diocese of Gloucester is newly drawn up from materials collected by the late Rev. Mr. Furney and communicated by Mr. Rogers of Gloucester". A postscript to the preface (1783) is critical of Atkyns.

The *New History* has remained a standard work of reference. Its creator survived to see the opening year of the nineteenth century, "a man of the strictest honour and most inflexible integrity", says his memorial in Cirencester church.

Publications: *The History of Fairford Church*, 1763 (10th edn., 1785 and later editions to 1841 include an account of the town of Fairford); *The History of the Parish and Abbey of Hayles- in Gloucestershire*, 1768; *A New History of Gloucestershire*, 1779 (reissued 1976, with an Introduction by Dr. N.M. Herbert); *History and Antiquities of Cirencester*, 1780 (2nd edn., with plates and plans added, 1800); *History and Antiquities of Gloucester*, 1781. The latter books are in the main extracts from the *New History*.

MSS. 1. By his will of 9 Dec, 1800 (P.R.O., Prob. 11/1355), Samuel Rudder bequeathed all his papers relating to the *New History*, including his "book of proof sheets with MS. notes in the margin", to his son Samuel, a steel button-maker in Birmingham. The book of proof sheets, with many interesting MS. notes, some personal, is now in the Gloucester Reference Library, having been presented by a direct descendant of the historian. At least two of Rudder's MS. note-books are still in his family: one, entitled 'Gloucestershire General History, No. 1', is in Australia; the other, 'Gloucestershire 18', containing lists of subscribers, corrections and additions to Atkyns, history notes for parishes A to Mangotsfield, etc., is owned by Major L.J.V. Rudder of Bibury, Glos.[6]

2. Other MS. remains of Rudder are:–
Glos. Coll., 88: printed questionnaire with MS additions (sent to Matthew Hale of Alderley, 4.4.1769).
Glos. Coll., 11492: autograph letters of Samuel, among papers relating to the sale of his father's property.
G.R.O., D421 E27. Draft history of Lydney parish, submitted to Bathurst family of Lydney, n.d.
Bodl., MSS. Phillipps-Robinson e. 117: memorials, c. 1780 - 94, in Cirencester church (8ff. in back of cash book). Formerly Phillipps Collection 13525.

Biographical sources: *D.N.B.*: *Gent. Mag*, 1801(i), 285 (obit.); *Glos. N. & Q.*,1, 184 - 5 and 2, 14 - 15, 80 - 82; Roland Austin,

'Samuel Rudder', in *N. & Q.*, ser. 11, iii, 244 (correction of *D.N.B.*), 1911; and 'Samuel Rudder', in *The Library*, July 1915; N.M. Herbert, *Introduction* to the re-issue of *The New History of Gloucestershire*, 1976.

Notes.
1. The date of his baptism at Uley is 5 Dec. 1726, though his memorial at Cirencester gives his birth as 26 December.
2. Samuel (*New History*, p.16) says: "I have foolishly followed them".
3. Presentment at Glos. Quarter Sessions, 10 Jan. 1757 (Plate II in *Gloucestershire Quarter Sessions Archives*, 1958).
4. On 31 July 1778 Rudder had written to a friend, Dr. Jones: "Gloucestershire is at length finished ....", sending him the Preface for his comments (Autograph letter interleaved in Gloucester Library proof sheets volume of the *New History*).
5. E.g. his remarks on 'Cowley' (Coaley): "The public roads here are the worst that can be conceived; and the poor labouring people are so abandoned to nastiness that they throw everything within a yard or two of their doors, where the filth makes a putrid stench, to the injury of their own health, and the annoyance of travellers, if any come among them. The better houses are gone to ruin, and there is not a gentleman resident in the parish; but this is not peculiar to Cowley".
6. I am indebted to Major Rudder for allowing me to see and use his extensive notes on Samuel Rudder and the family.

15. William BARRETT, ?1727 - 1789

The first historian of Bristol, William Barrett, was a medical man whose leisure occupation was local history. Having qualified as a surgeon in 1755, he lived and practised in Bristol for about thirty years. In 1775 he was elected an F.S.A. In the preface to his only book, he describes his handicaps:—

"Twenty years have elapsed since collections for the design were sought for .... and some progress made in compiling it .... but the author, receiving no encouragement to proceed .... desisted from the undertaking, locking up his papers for several years. .... Retiring from business into the country and often confined by the gout, he .... resumed the long intermitted task."

He also gives his reasons for steering a middle course between a work so prolix as to appeal only to scholars and one of too popular a kind. As early as August 1760, in a respectful letter to the Mayor and Corporation of Bristol, he had written:

".... having great materials for such a work by me & continually adding to my store, I have been induc'd to proceed in a work so large and of such difficulty from a desire of raising out of obscurity the history and antiquities of our flourishing City . . . and as I am in great want of some records out of the Chamber which wou'd throw new lights upon some obscure parts of the history, I hope that favour will not be deny'd me."[1]

In the end, the *History and Antiquities of Bristol,* which Barrett had described as an amusement rather than a labour or study,[2] appeared in print only in the year of his death. His obituary in the *Gentleman's Magazine* reminded readers "in excuse for its many inaccuracies" that nothing had ever before been published on the subject. The book, though well produced and illustrated, lacks an index, and criticism was aroused, in particular, because its author had accepted as genuine the historical fabrications of his friend Thomas Chatterton, the poet. But he had sought diligently for local records.

A portrait of William Barrett at the age of 31, engraved by Walker from a painting by Rymsdick, is sometimes found added as a frontispiece to his *History.* The *D.N.B.* gives his year of birth as 1733, but Miss Mary Williams, Bristol City Archivist, has now found his baptism at Lacock, Wilts. on 6 June 1729; and his apprenticeship, in Bristol City records, to a barber-surgeon for 7 years in 1744.

He retired to Wraxall, Somerset, but died in October 1789 while on a visit to his son, the Rev. W.T. Barrett, at High Ham, Somerset, and is buried there. His Will (P.R.O., Prob 11/1188/58) written in his own hand in September 1787, shows that he scarcely expected to see his work in print, for he asks his son and son-in-law "to transcribe for the press my History of Bristol .... then open subscriptions for printing it or sell the copy to a London bookseller . . .". An addition to his wife's memorial in St. Mary Redcliffe Church, Bristol, gives his age at death as 62.

Publication: History and Antiquities of Bristol, 1789.

MSS. In B.R.O., Ashton Court Records, AC/F 9/4 and AC/C 118, there are several letters from Barrett to members of the Smith family, referring to his antiquarian interests, 1765-88.

In his preface, Barrett wrote:- "The original deeds and copies collected for this history (many by the late Mr. Alexander Morgan) have been procured with so much labour, it would be a great loss to have them dispersed; it is intended therefore to lodge them in some public repository, probably the Bristol Library." His death so soon after publication probably frustrated his intention. Samuel Seyer, in the preface to his own Bristol history, says that he preserved many of Barrett's papers. These may be the deeds, etc. which were later acquired by G.W. Braikenridge, and most of which are now in the Bristol Record Office (see No. 24). Few, if any, of Barrett's own memoranda appear to have survived.

Biographical Sources: *D.N.B.*; *Biog. Suppt.*; *Gent. Mag.*, lvi (1786), correspondence between Barrett and Andrew Coltée Ducarel, antiquary, 1772; *Gent. Mag.* lix (1789), 921-24 (review) and 1052 (obit.).

Notes. 1. 4 Aug. 1760 (tracing in Bristol Ref. Library, Braikenridge Coll., v.1.17).
2. Letter to A.C. Ducarel, 1772 (see *Biog.sources*).

16. Thomas RUDGE, 1753 - 1825

Although he was a prominent Gloucestershire cleric and the author of three fairly well known Gloucestershire books, it is surprisingly hard to gain any impression of Thomas Rudge's personality. But his bold and confident signatures in his parish registers, and his elevation to the responsible duties of an archdeaconry, suggest that he was by no means a nonentity. He was certainly a worker.

His father and namesake was presumably the Thomas Rudge whose memorial on the north aisle wall of Gloucester cathedral describes him as attorney-at-law and Deputy [Diocesan] Registrar; he was also under-sheriff of the City of Gloucester. A younger son of his, the Rev. James Rudge, became both a Doctor of Divinity and a Fellow of the Royal Society. The elder son, Thomas, christened in St. Mary de Lode church, Gloucester, on 13 June 1753,[1] was entered at the King's (Cathedral) School in July 1759, went thence to Merton College, Oxford, and returned to spend his days in his native county, at first as curate at Frampton-on-Severn (1773). From 1784 he held the rectories of St. Michael, Gloucester and the rural parish of Haresfield, in plurality, for forty and forty-two years respectively. In 1814, at the age of sixty, he became Archdeacon of Gloucester, and in 1817 also Chancellor of Hereford Diocese. He is buried in Haresfield church.[2]

Meanwhile, in his more leisured years, Thomas Rudge had produced, between 1803 and 1811, a county history, a survey of Gloucestershire agriculture, and a history of Gloucester City. To do him justice, he made little claim to originality, saying in his preface to the county history that he, professing "merely to compress the matter of Sir Robert Atkyns into a narrower compass and fill up the interval of the last century, claims no merit for any laborious investigation of ancient records." He adds, rather ruefully, that (as others have found) "the difficulty of procuring information is greater than may generally be imagined". Rudge refers to himself throughout as "the Editor". The books were, in fact, handy and more popular epitomes of the ponderous folios of Atkyns and Rudder, and as such proved useful to a wider public.[3] On the other hand, Rudge's *General View of the Agriculture of the County* was one of a series of county surveys commissioned by the old Board of Agriculture, and although it was doubtless a revision of the *General View* written by George Turner in 1794, and both must have owed much to the eminent William Marshall's *Rural Economy of Gloucestershire* (1789), it is still exceptional that a clergyman should have been invited (by the Board which Marshall himself had created) to undertake such a task. Perhaps he had been exceptionally successful in farming his glebe at Haresfield. His survey has no preface nor apparently any personal allusions to the writer.

Publications: *The History of the County of Gloucester, compressed and brought down to the year 1803*, 1803; *A General View of the Agriculture of the County of Gloucester*, 1807; *History and Antiquities of Gloucester* [city], 1811.

MSS: None known.

Biographical sources: *D.N.B.*; *Gent. Mag.*, 1825 (ii), 474; John Donaldson, *Agricultural Biography*, 93; ordination papers etc. in Gloucester Diocesan Archives, E 1 (in G.R.O.)

Notes.
1. Not, as stated in the *D.N.B.*, 1754. I have to thank Mr. Brian Frith for finding this entry in the parish register.
2. M.I. on floor of nave, copied by J.D.T. Niblett — see Canon Bazeley's notes in Glos. Coll. 6, vol. 1, 290.
3. For Fosbroke's comments, however, see Introduction, p. 23.

17. Samuel SEYER, 1757 - 1831

Another not untypical antiquary from a clerical and academic background, the Reverend Samuel Seyer, was the son of Samuel, Rector of St. Michael's, Bristol and Master of Bristol Grammar School. Samuel, junior (M.A., of Corpus Christi, Oxon.), was Master of the Royal Fort School, Bristol from 1790 to 1810, and Rector of Horfield, 1813 - 28 and of Filton, 1824 - 31, both in south Gloucestershire. He was also chaplain to the Bishop of Bristol,

In the preface to his *Charters .... of Bristol* (1812), he refers to his intended history of the city, which was eventually issued in four parts between 1822 and 1825. It professed to be brought "down to the present time", but in fact does not go beyond 1760. Seyer's preface, long-winded but of considerable interest, refers to his friendship with William Barrett, who died when Seyer was 32, but with whom he had been "in the constant habit of conversation". He puts on record that he rescued many of Barrett's papers and documents after his death, and that he called his own book 'Memoirs' so as not to conflict with Barrett's 'History'. No doubt Seyer's scholarly equipment was sounder than that of Barrett; he was a linguist, and the *D.N.B.* calls him painstaking and learned.

Seyer's notes on the topography of Bristol, for a continuation of his book which he did not achieve, have survived (see below). His memorial[1] is in Shirehampton church, and there is a portrait of him by Nathan Branwhite, engraved by Walker, as well as a mezzotint, drawn and engraved by William Petter.

Publications: *Charters & Letters Patent granted to the Town and City of Bristol*, 1812; *Memoirs, historical and topographical, of Bristol and its neighbourhood, from the earliest period down to the present time*, 1822 - 25.

MSS. 1. B.R.O., 12147: personal papers, deeds, etc, with memoranda, correspondence and accounts relating to the *Memoirs .... of Bristol*, 1821 - 25.
    2. Bris. L., Jefferies Collection: notes on Bristol topography, for a second part of the *Memoirs*, with some original collected records. (Bound in 2 vols.)

Biographical sources: *D.N.B*; *Gent. Mag.*, ci (1831), 471 - 2 (obit.)

Notes.   1.   For text of inscription see *Glos. N. & Q.*, 2, 392. It gives his age as 73.

18. George Worrall COUNSEL, 1758 - 1843

Counsel's history of the City of Gloucester (1829), produced fairly late in his long life, at a time when Gloucester was growing, is of modest size, but it makes a useful supplement to the more erudite histories by the two clerics, Archdeacon Rudge and the Rev. T.D. Fosbroke, which had appeared in 1811 and 1819 respectively.

Its author, an attorney and alderman of Gloucester, was more conscious than his forerunners of current or recent events. He was a friend of Jemmy Wood, the Gloucester banker and miser, who left him £10,000; intimate also with Fosbroke, who in the preface to his own History of Gloucester thanks Counsel for his help.[1] Fosbroke prints a brief pedigree of the Counsel family, which shows that G.W. Counsel's father was Joshua, a Gloucester surgeon, and his mother Anne, daughter of David Gardner, a Stroud clothier. Like several Gloucester antiquaries, he went to the King's (Cathedral) School, Gloucester.

Counsel's fellow-citizens were well aware of his antiquarian tastes. His obituary in the *Gloucester Journal* refers to "papers communicated to periodicals and our own columns, which abound with them .... No one thought of covering up a tesselated pavement .... or even disposing of a coin, without first submitting it to his examination .... His memory was most retentive, and he retained his faculties to the last." In later years he had correspondence with Sir Thomas Phillipps, and sold him documents.[2] It may be added that he had a hobby of lampooning his fellow Town Councillors and others in doggerel verse.

Publications: 'The Old Church of St. Mary de Lode, Gloucester', in *Gent. Mag.*, 1826 (ii), 505 - 06; *The History and Description of the City of Gloucester, from the earliest period to the present time*, 1829; biographical memoir of John Corbet, prefixed to a reprint of Corbet's tract *Self-imployment in Secret*, 1835; *Some Account of the Life and Martyrdom of John Hooper, D.D. .... with an appendix containing the history of the Bishoprick of Gloucester*, 1840.

MSS. It seems from correspondence in Bodl. MSS. Phillipps-Robinson, 1833 - 1843 (b. 146, fol. 114, and c. 484, fols. 246 - 9), between Counsel's executors and Sir Thomas Phillips in 1843, that at least some of Counsel's papers were sold to Phillipps. At all events, correspondence, documents, and historical memoranda of G.W. Counsel, over 160 items, mostly of 1820-36 dates, including letters of T.D. Fosbroke and John Britton, were sold at Sotheby's from the Phillipps Collection on 14 June 1971 (lot 1506), and resold by the London dealer Stanley Crowe; their present whereabouts is not known. Crowe's catalogue no. 83 (1973), of which G.R.O. has a copy, gives some details.

There are several letters written by Counsel to Phillipps between 1833 and 1841 in Bodl. MSS. Phillipps-Robinson, b. 136 and c. 446, 451 and 474. I am indebted to Mr. Timothy Rogers of the Bodleian for bringing these to my attention.

Biographical sources: T.D. Fosbroke, *History of the City of Gloucester*, preface; *Gloucester Journal*, 28 Jan. 1843 (obit.); correspondence (as above) in Bodleian Library.

Notes. 1. "G.W. Counsel, Esq. permitted his most rare and valuable tracts to be reprinted. No man is equally versed in the antiquities of the City." On 27 July 1818, in a letter to his publisher J.B. Nichols, Fosbroke had mentioned, more colloquially, "Mr. Counsel, an opulent sollicitor, very fond of antiquities".
2. See Illus. 18 and 32. Writing to Sir Thomas in 1834, Mr. John Higford, of Newark House, Gloucester, calls Counsel "a very particular old gentleman", who was quite willing to lend manuscripts but most reluctant to part with them.

19. Daniel LYSONS, 1762 - 1834

The Lysons family,[1] which contributed two distinguished brothers to the roll of Gloucestershire antiquaries, had been of yeoman status in the county by the 16th century and established at Hempsted Court, on the outskirts of Gloucester, as lessees from about 1630 and owners from the early eighteen-hundreds. For five generations the eldest son had been given the name Daniel, but the Reverend Daniel Lysons, born in 1762, was the eldest son of a younger son, Samuel, Rector of Rodmarton near Cirencester. Educated at Bath Grammar School and Oxford, Daniel succeeded his father in the family living of Rodmarton, and held it from 1804 unil 1833.

While previously holding curacies in Surrey, he had begun his survey of the environs of London, and Horace Walpole, whose domestic chaplain he became, encouraged his interests in history and topography. He was elected F.S.A. in 1790. In collaboration with his brother Samuel (No. 20) he began work on *Magna Britannia*, which was intended to be a survey of England — a latter day Camden's *Britannia*. They covered ten counties alphabetically from Bedfordshire to Devon, but after Samuel's death in 1819 Daniel did not have the heart to pursue the enterprise. He himself died at Hempsted Court, which he had inherited in 1800, but was buried at Rodmarton. His portrait by Lawrence was in 1868 in the possession of his eldest son Canon Samuel Lysons, himself a minor antiquarian writer and Rector of Rodmarton from 1833 to 1877. There is also an engraving from a chalk drawing, and a pencil sketch in the Society of Antiquaries Library.[2]

Daniel Lysons, unfortunately not having reached Gloucestershire in the alphabetical survey of England, does not seem to have concerned himself much with his own county. His *Environs of London* and the unfinished *Magna Britannia* are, however, standard works held in high repute.

Publications: *The Environs of London*, 1792 - 96; *Magna Britannia* (unfinished, see above), 6 vols., 1806 - 22; *History of the origin and progress of the meeting of the Three Choirs .... and of the Charity connected with it*, 1812; *A Sketch of the Life and Character of the late C.B. Trye*, 1812 (30pp); *Revenues of the Parochial Clergy*, 1824.

MSS. 1. B.L. Add. 9408 - 9471: correspondence, collections and drawings, relating to the *Magna Britannia, Environs of London,* etc. Gloucestershire is very scantily represented. 2. Yale University, U.S.A., Lindsay Fleming Collection ('Lysons Boxes'): correspondence of Samuel and Daniel Lysons, some relating to Gloucestershire.

Biographical sources: *D.N.B.*; obituary in *Annual Biography*, xix, 103 - 09; 'The Lysons Family', in *Glos. N. & Q.*, 2, 533 - 5; pedigree and note in *TBGAS*, lxxxi, 212 - 3.

Notes. 1. The name is earlier found spelt Lysance or Lysaunce.
2. MS. 782/9

20. Samuel LYSONS, 1763 - 1819

Samuel, the younger son of the Reverend Samuel Lysons, was sent to the Grammar School at Bath with his brother Daniel, and was then articled to a solicitor instead of going to the University. He was entered at the Inner Temple in 1784, and practised at the Bar, but like his brother turned his attention to historical research, becoming an F.S.A. at the age of twenty-three.[1] His miscellany of drawings published in 1791 - 2 and some surviving manuscript notes show that by 1785 he was actively studying Gloucestershire antiquities, not only in books but at first hand.

Within a few years Samuel Lysons, mainly self-schooled so far as one can tell, developed into a field-archaeologist much ahead of his time in discernment and technique. His report of 1797 on his excavation of the palatial Roman mansion at Woodchester near Stroud, sumptuously printed, established his reputation. In the same year he was elected to the Fellowship of the Royal Society. He was Director of the Society of Antiquaries from 1798 to 1809, a Vice-President from 1812, Vice-President and Treasurer of the Royal Society from 1810, and Antiquary to the Royal Academy from 1818. His *magnum opus was the Reliquiae Britannico-Romanae*, a survey of sites and finds in Roman Britain,[2] published in instalments between 1801 and 1817 and lavishly illustrated in colour, like the Woodchester book. Worn out by his exertions, mental and physical, he died when only fifty-six.

From 1803 Lysons had been Keeper of the Public Records, then in the Tower of London, a position which must have been of great advantage to his brother and himself in their great enterprise of the *Magna Britannia* (see under Daniel Lysons). Private means, to be sure, enabled them to devote time and money to their pursuits, but Samuel was undoubtedly a man of exceptional energy and intellectual power. Like Daniel, he was also an artist of some talent, exhibiting at the Royal Academy from 1785 to 1801. All the plates in his *Woodchester* and his *Gloucestershire Antiquities* (1803) were etched by himself from his own drawings. In the intervals of his archaeological field-work he wrote 28 papers for *Archaeologia* (Vols. IX to XIX), and also printed, anonymously, some early proceedings in Chancery from the public records.

The striking portrait of Samuel Lysons by Sir Thomas Lawrence has been reproduced from an engraving more than once.[3] His portrait was also painted by George Dance, junior, and by Francis Newton.

Publications: *Etchings of Views and Antiquities in the County of Gloucester*, 1791 - 96[4]; *An Account of Roman Antiquities discovered at Woodchester* ...., 1797; *A Collection of Gloucestershire Antiquities*, 1803 - 04; *Reliquiae Britannico-Romanae*, 1801 - 1817 (3 vols.); *An Account of the* .... *Roman Villa discovered at Bignor, Sussex*, 1815; papers reprinted from *Archaeologia* relating to Roman discoveries at Combend Farm (in Elkstone), 1789; Quenington church, 1792; tombs in Tewkesbury Abbey church, 1801; a wall-painting in Cirencester church, 1806; and the Great Witcombe Roman villa, 1818 - 19.

MSS. 1.Glos. Coll., 39. Small portfolio of historical and topographical notes and sketches for the etchings in *Gloucestershire Antiquities* (1803).
 2. Glos. Coll., 42 and 44. Original drawings, 77 in all, formerly owned by H.W. Bruton of Gloucester and sold at Sotheby's, June 1921. These are inserted in copies of Lysons's *Etchings and Views* .... (1791) and *Gloucestershire Antiquities*.
 3. Glos. Coll., 280. Exercise book dated 1785, containing memoranda, notes on stained glass, list of topographical engravings, etc.
 4. Glos. Coll., 663. Original drawings of 33 Gloucestershire churches, c. 1790 - 1803, unpublished.
 5. Glos. Coll., 9668. Note on Calcot barn, with plan, 1795.
 6. Glos. Coll., 12281. Extracts from an unpublished history of the Berkeley family. The MS. was sold at Sotheby's, with Canon Samuel Lysons's library, in July 1880 (see *N. & Q.*, ser. 11, xi, 271 and the *Biog. Suppt.*)[5]
 7. Soc. of Ant., Lysons. About 160 architectural drawings, presented to the Society in 1882 by Sir A.W. Franks, later P.S.A.
 8. Soc. of Ant. MS. 782. Family papers including letters and memoranda by Samuel Lysons, sen., and portfolio containing many original drawings, not all published in *Etchings of Views and Antiquities*.
 9. B.L. Add. 9408 - 9471. Correspondence etc., - see Daniel Lysons (No. 19) to whom this mostly relates.
 10. Yale University, U.S.A. Correspondence, - see Daniel Lysons.

Biographical sources: D.N.B.; Gent. Mag., 1819, 273 - 5 (obituary) and Oct. 1823, 303 - 04; *Archaeologia,* LXII (1910), 70 - 71, with portrait; *Man. G. Lit. and Biog. Suppt.;* Lindsay Fleming, *Memoir and Select Letters of Samuel Lysons* (privately printed), 1924; Dame Joan Evans, *A History of the Society of Antiquaries,* 1956. See also sources for Daniel Lysons. A full length biography of Samuel Lysons has yet to be written.

Notes.
1. "an excitable and vigorous west-countryman, with a loud voice that made his emphatic statements seem blunter and his views more extreme than they were" (Joan Evans, *Hist. of the Soc. of Antiquaries,* p. 187). Some crotchety fellow-Antiquaries found Lysons too masterful for their taste.
2. Vol. II includes 33 plates of Roman antiquities found in Gloucestershire.
3. E.g., in Joan Evans's *History of the Society of Antiquaries,* Plate XXIV.
4. Issued by instalments, and some included in *A Collection of Gloucestershire Antiquities* (1803). The complicated bibliographical story is told in the *Man. G. Lit.* and the *Glos. Coll. Catalogue.*
5. A long quarrel between two architects and Fellows of the Society of Antiquaries, James Wyatt and John Carter, was finally quelled by Lysons, who read chapters of his Berkeley history to the Society at *fifteen* meetings when lack of other business might have given an opportunity for acrimonious disputes. (See Joan Evans, *op. cit.* p. 213)

21. James DALLAWAY, 1763 - 1834

James Dallaway, a learned and versatile writer, was a Gloucestershire man who published scarcely anything in his own name on his own county. Born in Bristol, he was a son of James Dallaway of Painswick and nephew of William Dallaway, an 'eminent clothier' of Brimscombe and High Sheriff of Gloucestershire in 1766. After Cirencester Grammar School and Trinity, Oxford, the younger James was ordained and became curate of Rodborough, near Stroud, in 1787, though he seems to have lived mostly in Gloucester. While there he was employed in editing Ralph Bigland's history of the county (published 1791) after Bigland's death in 1784.[1] He was elected F.S.A. in 1789, and also studied medicine, taking an Oxford M.B. in 1794. Meanwhile he had written the introduction to *A Collection of the Coats of Arms borne by the Nobility and Gentry of Gloucestershire*, published anonymously in 1792, perhaps written by Sir George Nayler, Garter King of arms, a native of Stroud (but cf. the *D.N.B.*'s doubts); and a book of his own on heraldry followed in 1793, with a dedication to the 11th Duke of Norfolk.

It must have been through the patronage either of the Duke or of the Earl (later 1st Marquess) of Bute that Dallaway was appointed in 1794 chaplain and physician to the British Embassy in Turkey. Although his stay in Constantinople lasted only some eighteen months, he paid a long visit to Italy on his way home, and these experiences did much to broaden his interests. A book on Turkey (1797) was followed in 1800 by one on architecture, sculpture and painting, and he contemplated attempting a history of the Ottoman Empire. On his return to England, in January 1797, he became secretary to the Earl Marshal (the Duke of Norfolk), a position which he held for the remainder of his life. The Duke also procured for him in 1803 the vicarage of Slinfold, Sussex, and in 1801 he had been installed as Vicar of Leatherhead in Surrey, where he lived thenceforth, holding both livings and from 1811 a prebend in Chichester Cathedral.

In the same year he undertook a *History of West Sussex*, which appeared in two imposing volumes in 1815 and 1819, but was criticized for many careless mistakes; the author, in fact, with his writing on literature and art, had too many distractions to be a conscientious historian. In later years his interest in the West Country revived, with his papers on Bristol history which are listed below.

The antiquary Joseph Hunter (1783 - 1861), in notes now in the British Library,[2] describes his introduction to James Dallaway in May 1830:– "I found a fine, hearty-looking, gentlemanly man, full of conversation, little short of seventy; having lived much in the world, known many remarkable persons ...." But in a later note Hunter records how he was told "a long history of Mr. Dallaway", — how he was disappointed of an Oxford fellowship, in love, and in ecclesiastical preferment, "and this has somewhat soured him, as his friends say." In his *Anecdotes of the Arts in England*, Dallaway refers to Gloucester as "a city where I once resided, and which is endeared to me by the experience of the most cordial and active friendship, and by attachments which will cease only with my life." In 1820, however, he wrote to Daniel Lysons: "I am a 'banished man' from Gloucestershire, — and indeed have survived those who most attached me to it".

Publications (in addition to minor papers): *Inquiries into the Origin and Progress of the Science of Heraldry in England*, 1793; *Constantinople, Ancient and Modern* (etc), 1797; *Anecdotes of the Arts in England ....*, 1800; *Letters and other works of Lady Mary Wortley Montagu* (ed.), 1803; *Observations on English Architecture*, (etc), 1806; *History of the Western Division of the County of Sussex*, 1815 - 19; *Statuary and Sculpture among the Ancients*, 1816; *Horace Walpole's Anecdotes of Painting* (ed.), 1826 - 28; *William Wyrcestre Redivivus*, 1823[3], *ntiquities of Bristow in the Middle Centuries* (reprints of earlier papers on Bristol), 1834.

MSS. 1. In 1887 a correspondent, 'C.S.B.G.', in *Glos. N. & Q.*, 3, 119, said that his maternal grandmother was James Dallaway's sister [Martha Best] and that many manuscripts of Dallaway's were in his possession. This correspondent must have been Clement S.B. Gardner, son of Martha's daughter Sophia, who married Sankey Gardner; so that the MSS. were doubtless the records of the Best, Gardner and Dallaway families which were sold by Frank Hammond, the Sutton Coldfield bookseller, in 1966, and are now in the West Sussex Record Office.[4]

2. Letters of Dallaway (whereabouts now unknown) were in the collection of the late Lindsay Fleming[5]; others are in the Wilmarth S. Lewis collection in the U.S.A., in the Petworth

House archives, at the College of Arms, at Preston Park, Brighton (Thomas Stanford MSS., L/Z/16), and elsewhere.
3. 'A Journey from Rodborough to Gloucester, with description of the Country and an account of the Cathedral', in MS., was in 1842 owned by J. Delafield Phelps (No. 22), — see his *Col lectanea Gloucestriensia*. The Gloucester City Librarian states that there are no manuscripts among the Clifford (ex Phelps) books now lodged with the Library.

Biographical sources: *D.N.B.*; obituary in *Gent. Mag.*, n.s. ii (1834), 318 - 20; F.W. Steer, 'Memoir and Letters of James Dallaway, 1763-1834', in *Sussex Archaeological collections*, Vol. CIII (1965), and 'A Postscript', in Vol. CV (1967); Irvine Gray, 'James Dallaway', in *TBGAS*, lxxxi, 208 - 10.

Notes. 1. Dallaway writes, in a letter to his friend and exact contemporary Samuel Lysons dated 31 May 1791 (Lindsay Flemming Coll.): "The references you have made to our publication deserve the best thanks both Mr. Bigland [i.e. Richard Bigland] and myself ...." The full letter is given in Dr. F.W. Steer's *Memoir* (see *Biographical sources*), p.3.
2. Add. MSS. 36527.
3. 'Notices of ancient church architecture in the 15th century, particularly in Bristol, with hints for practicable restorations', preceded by an entertaining conversation with the amiable spectre of William Worcestre.
4. These include interesting letters from James Dallaway written on his way to and from Turkey in 1794 - 5 and while there.
5. Many, fortunately, printed in the very full *Memoir* by my friend the late Dr. Francis Steer, F.S.A., to which this brief summary of Dallaway's life is much indebted.

22. John Delafield PHELPS
1764 or 5 - 1842

J.D. Phelps was a barrister who had inherited wealth from his father, also John Delafield Phelps, esquire, of Dursley, High Sheriff of Gloucestershire in 1761.[1] The son was Lord of the Manor of Dursley, but for many years lived, as a lessee, at the well-known 15th century manor-house of Chavenage, near Tetbury. He had been at Oriel, Oxford, and Lincoln's Inn, and was an Exchequer Bill Loan Commissioner.

In his leisure, which may have been considerable, Phelps made a notable collection of Gloucestershire books, pamphlets, prints and coins. In his time the chapel of Chavenage House was used also as a chapel-of-ease for that part of Horsley parish; and the chaplain, the Rev. — Panton, compiled a catalogue of the Phelps collection, which was printed in 1842 under the title of *Collectanea Glocestriensia*. The collection, which included many rarities, descended through a nephew, William Phelps (d. 1906) to Major A.W. Clifford of Dursley, both of whom added to it. Much of the local material is now deposited with the Gloucester Reference Library.

J.D. Phelps was elected F.S.A. in 1800, and F.R.S. in 1815. He was an original member of the Roxburghe Club, "an ardent bibliophile, and a great investigator and accumulator of antiquities", says a contributor to *N. & Q.*, adding that he collected "a great mass of material for the elucidation of the history, antiquities etc., of Gloucestershire", If any of this was manuscript, its present whereabouts is unknown. Canon Samuel Lysons (nephew of the more famous Samuel) refers to Phelps as a friend. He died at Chavenage in December 1842.

Publications: none (but see above).

MSS. There appear to be none among the Phelps Collection now in the Gloucester Library.

Biographical sources: *Gent. Mag.*, 1843 (1), 219; *N. & Q.*, ser. 1, v, 346, vi, 107; Glos. Coll. Cat., 2092.

Note.   1.   As with so many of the later Gloucestershire gentry, the Phelps family's fortunes were founded on cloth. Having married into the ancient family of Field, of Field Place in

Paganhill (Stroud), they transmuted Field into Delafield. (See *V.C.H., Glos,* xi, 118, and Dr. Jennifer Tann's paper 'Some Account Books of the Phelps Family of Dursley', in *TBGAS*, lxxxvi, 107 - 17. .

23. Thomas Dudley FOSBROKE, 1770 - 1842

An antiquary of considerable learning and prodigious industry, the Reverend T.D. Fosbroke, has left a variety of printed works, while many of his manuscript notes and transcripts have also survived, though dispersed and confusing.

The son of William Fosbrooke[1] of London, he went from St. Paul's School to Pembroke College, Oxford, and started his Gloucestershire researches while curate of Horsley (1794 - 1810) By 1800 or earlier he had embarked on the work which appeared in 1807 with the typically ponderous and censorious title *Abstract of records and manuscripts respecting the County of Gloucester: formed into a history, correcting the very erroneous accounts, and supplying numerous deficiencies in Sir R. Atkins and subsequent writers*. Unluckily for him, Fosbroke had been forestalled by Rudge,[2] whose two-volume county history was published in 1803, so he hastily issued the preliminary part of his own book, 96 pages only, in the same year (and by the same printers), as a *History of Gloucestershire, genealogical and statistical*. Fosbroke's *History of the City of Gloucester* (1819) was largely based on the unpublished MSS. of Bigland, and was the first serious attempt at a full-length account of the city which, unlike Furney's, got into print.

Fosbroke, always given to sharp criticism of other writers and peevish grumbling about his own misfortunes, complains in a letter of December 1803 to his friend Robert Hughes[3]:

> "The encouragement I receive is but scanty and the expence of the times still more unfavourable .... The labour and perplexity is enormous .... I am plagued to death with the details of business in addition to the work, which my various agents &c absolutely contrive to make a species of persecution."

Although disappointed with the reception of his works, and his failure to get assistance from the Royal Literary Fund, he persevered for many years with research and miscellaneous publications, both general and local. In the preface to the second edition of his *British Monachism*, he replies thus to criticism by John Britton:

> "When this gent. knows that the author studied archaeology 8 hours a

day for 18 years; has published a County History, classified a Dictionary of Arms, ... and finished an Encyclopaedia of Antiquities .... measuring two feet of quarto MS. in height, only one third of which was printed and a heavy pecuniary loss sustained .... perhaps he may think that a literary veteran, crippled by severe wounds, does not regard the scratch of a pin."

In 1825 he describes himself[4] as "now advanced in life, unbeneficed and unpatronized, with a wife and 7 children." He had in 1810 become curate and in 1830 was at last made Vicar of Walford, Herefordshire (then united with Ruardean, Glos.), holding the joint livings until his death in 1842. He is buried at Walford, where there is a memorial.[5]

Fosbroke was a student of archaeology and Anglo-Saxon, and contributed numerous reviews to the *Gentleman's Magazine*. His Gloucestershire history, as its title proclaims, is founded on painstaking documentary research, but he shows little interest in social or current affairs, except that some of the large-paper copies contain a 32pp. appendix on the 'Origin and History of the Manners and Customs of the inhabitants of Gloucestershire'.[6] For his rough notes he frequently used shorthand.

Publications: *British Monachism*, 1802; *Abstracts .... respecting the County of Gloucester* (for full title see above), 1807; *An original History of the City of Gloucester*, 1819, reprinted 1976 with Introduction by Peter Ripley; *Ariconensia* (about Ross-on-Wye, Ariconium, etc.), 1821; *Berkeley Manuscripts (Abstracts and extracts of Smyth's Lives of the Berkeleys, etc)*, 1821; *Encyclopaedia of Antiquities*, 1825; *A picturesque and topographical account of Cheltenham and its vicinity*, 1826; *Tourists' Grammar*, 1826; *Foreign Topography*, 1828. For a full bibliography of Fosbroke's works and pamphlets, see Roland Austin's paper listed below. As will be seen, he descended to popular guide-books.

MSS. 1. Fosbroke's manuscripts, which seem to have been mostly in volume form, were sold after his death to William Strong, a Bristol bookseller and uncle of William George (see No. 43), and resold with Strong's library at Sotheby's in 1847 at trifling prices, as is recorded by J.G. Nichols in a memorandum later printed as an appendix to Roland Austin's paper on Fosbroke's letters. The manuscripts thus dispersed included papers on the Clinton and Tankerville families (8 vols.); collections relating to Gloucestershire (2 vols.); notes on antiquities in Beds., Berks., Herefs., etc, with drawings; notes on Old English customs and Saxon terms; a list of obsolete words (1 vol.); memoranda on antiquities, etc. (?21 vols.; collections for the *Encyclopaedia of Antiquities* and *Foreign Topography* (14 vols.).

2. These and/or other Fosbroke MSS. were acquired by the omnivorous collector Sir Thomas Phillipps, whose Catalogue records: 7099 - 7111 'Autograph MSS of T.D. Fosbroke (12 vols.)'. From the detailed list it appears that only 7101 (for Bristol history), 7103 (Cheltenham tour), 7105 (descents of Glos. manors), 7106 (Thornbury manor customs), 7107 and 7108 (see below), 7110 (Glos. miscell.) and 7111 (Gloucester City) related to Gloucestershire or Bristol.

Phillipps also had 12341 (topographical antiquities), 13626 (see below), 14221 (18 vols. chiefly *Dictionary of Antiquities* notes), and 18205 - 22 (MSS. in shorthand, of which only 18206, Ruardean tithes, and some Gloucester city notes in 18220 concerned Glos.), — all apparently Fosbroke's.

Of the foregoing, 7107, 7108, 7111, 13626 and 18209 - 11 were sold at Sotheby's on 26 June 1967, and three vols. were in 1978 owned by Mr. D.C.C. Wilson of Swindon, Glos., who has kindly allowed them to be examined. These are :

> Ph. 7107, 'Vol. 10', containing transcripts of Glos. records, including 'John Smith's MSS. respecting estates connected with Berkeley Harnesse and the vicinity, *penes* the late Mr. Beel' [*recte* Veal]. Much shorthand is interspersed.
> Ph. 7108, 'Vol. 11', 'Collections on loose papers', bound now in a folio vol., a few memoranda etc. loose. List of subscribers and payments, draft parish histories, letters from informants including Robt. Hughes of Cheltenham[3] and Wm. Davies of Eastington, c. 1802 - 05.
> Ph. 13626, marked 'Boone' in pencil on fly-leaf. (Boone was a London bookseller patronized by Phillipps). 'Collections relative to Glos.' Apparently the semi-final drafts of Fosbroke's county history, with amendments and additions. Arranged by Hundreds, some parishes marked 'complete'. (folio vol.)

Eight more Fosbroke vols. were sold in another Phillipps sale at Sotheby's on 26 June 1974 (lot 2921), but only Ph. 12341 (see above) related to Glos.

3. The Gloucester Library has a large number of Fosbroke's

letters, viz. (i) Glos. Coll. 101, relating to a subscription for his country history, 1803 - 07 (5 docs.); and (ii) Glos. Coll. 12752, between Fosbroke and his publishers, Messrs. Nichols, 1796 - 1841, with others relating to his affairs, 1842 - 47 (428 docs.) Considerable extracts from these are in print (see below).
4. Nottingham University Dept. of MSS., Clumber MSS. Cat., p. 71 (N.R.A. 7411): Records & MSS. of the Clinton family, compiled by T.D. Fosbroke [for the Duke of Newcastle], 1 vol.
5. Yale Univy., U.S.A., Osborn Coll., c.230 (N.R.A. 18661): 3 note-books, part holograph, c. 1788 - 89 (no details in catalogue).
6. G.R.O. has stray Fosbroke letters in several collections.

Biographical sources: D.N.B.; family history in Fosbroke's *Encycl. of Antiquities* (prefixed to Vol. I), *British Monachism*, 3rd edn., pp. 14 - 23, with a portrait (*aet.* 46) and *Ariconensia*, pp. 168 - 183, with some autobiographical notes; *Glos. N. & Q.*, 4, 622 - 5; *Gent. Mag.*, 1819(2), 521 - 2 (review) and 1842 (1), 214 - 6 (obit.); Roland Austin, 'Letters of T.D. Fosbroke', in *TBGAS*, xxxvii, 135 - 184, with bibliography.

Notes.
1. T.D. Fosbrooke changed the spelling of his name to Fosbroke in 1820, 'in true antiquarian spirit' — so he writes in a letter to Nichols — having found in his genealogical researches that his ancestors usually spelt it with one O. See Austin, *loc. cit. supra.*
2. See Introduction, p. 23.
3. A Cheltenham solicitor of antiquarian leanings.
4. *Encycl. of Antiquities*, preface.
5. Copy in Glos. Coll. 12757.
6. *Man. G. Lit.*, I, 55 - 6.

24. George Weare BRAIKENRIDGE, 1775 - 1856

Perhaps G.W. Braikenridge (F.S.A., 1827), who appears to have written little or nothing, ranks as a collector and dilettante rather than as a serious antiquary, but he certainly left his mark in Bristol. The son of a Virginia planter and merchant of Bristol origin, he was born in Hanover County, Virginia — then still a British colony — but was brought back to England by his loyalist family as a small child, and educated at Dr. Estlin's school in Bristol. He became senior partner in the West Indian firm of Braikenridge & Honnywill, retired from business when about forty-five, and settled at Broomwell House, Brislington, on the Somerset outskirts of Bristol. Here he collected everything concerning the city, — books, pamphlets, manuscripts and pictures; besides beetles, fossils, Tudor furniture and stained glass. A letter from the Elton family of Clevedon, Somerset, where he spent the summer months from 1836 onwards, gives some glimpses of the scene: "The Braikenridge family are particularly agreeable .... a splendid library[1] .... fine carving and painted glass in profusion, and a museum .... Old Mr. B. is a most benevolent man .... looking so young for his age." He possessed, we are told, a remarkable fund of local anecdote.

In the eighteen-twenties Braikenridge employed some of his considerable wealth in commissioning various local artists, including Hugh O'Neill (1784 - 1824)[2] to provide him with Bristol views, at first apparently with the intention of making a grangerised copy of Barrett's History. The result was a collection of over 1500 water-colours, now in the Bristol Art Gallery, — a unique record of the city and port in the early nineteenth century. Later, in order to illustrate Collinson's *History of Somerset*, he employed an artist for more than ten years to travel through the county and depict architectural features and antiquities.

G.W. Braikenridge took a leading part in building Christ Church, Clevedon, of which his son became the first vicar. His collections of manuscript and printed matter are now in the Bristol Record Office (over 200 medieval deeds) and Bristol Library (his antiquarian notes). A *Catalogue of the Library .... collected by George Weare Braikenridge*, 56 pages of which were devoted to

Bristol, was published in 1894 (50 copies only) and a *Calendar of Deeds, chiefly of Bristol, collected by G.W. Braikenridge*, in 1899.

Publications: none.

MSS. Antiquarian notes in Bristol Central Library, Braikenridge Coll.

Biographical sources: *Gent. Mag.* 1856 (i), memoir; *George Weare Braikenridge and his Collection,* by Marie-Christine Livingstone, Asst. Curator, Bristol City Art Gallery (synopsis of lecture).

Notes.
1. See James Dallaway's letter to Braikenridge, Illus. 21.
2. According to John Evans, *Chronological Outline of the History of Bristol*, p. 219, f.n., 435 drawings were by O'Neill (for whom see the *D.N.B.*)

25. Paul Hawkins FISHER, 1779 - 1873

Born in Stroud, the seventh son of Benjamin Fisher, a currier, Paul Hawkins Fisher attended the King's School (Cathedral or College School) in Gloucester and became an attorney in Stroud, in partnership with his brother Samuel. He took some part in public affairs in the town, but his interests do not seem to have extended much beyond the neighbourhood.

He edited and wrote much of the anonymous material for *The Gloucestershire Repository*, a periodical miscellany printed in Stroud in 1817 and 1822. This included his 'Three Weeks Tour into Wales' reprinted separately in 1818. After this nothing is heard of Fisher as a writer until the appearance of his one book, at first in serial form in the *Stroud Journal*, between 1860 and 1865, as *Reminiscences of Stroud and its Vicinity, by an Old Inhabitant* (he was already over eighty), and finally published in 1871 as *Notes and Recollections of Stroud*. The book contains a mass of information, much of it from personal memories of the author's long life, and is unusually rewarding for a local history of the nineteenth century. It was reprinted in 1891, with a few notes added by his son, and has again been re-issued in 1975, with a foreword by Dr. N.M. Herbert.

Fisher lived from 1809 at the house called The Castle in Stroud. There is a good photograph of him, at the age of 92, in his *Notes and Recollections*.

Publications: contributions to the *Gloucestershire Repository* (series 1, 1817 and series 2, 1822): *Notes and Recollections of Stroud* (see above), 1871, reprinted 1891 and 1975.

MSS. G.R.O., D1842, H 1 and 2: notes and correspondence on Stroud history (a small quantity only)

Glos. Coll.13442. Autograph letter (3pp.) from Fisher to W.H. Hyett of Painswick, on Robert Raikes and Sunday Schools.

Biographical sources: N.M. Herbert, *Foreword* to reprint of *Notes and Recollections of Stroud*; information from Mr. G.T. St. J. Sanders.

26. John EVANS, 1784 - 1831

Mr. Roy Hudleston, in a paper in the Bristol and Gloucestershire Archaeological Society's *Transactions* (see below), distinguishes this John Evans, schoolmaster and Presbyterian minister, from two contemporary Bristol namesakes, — John Evans (1774 - 1828),[1] printer and newspaper editor; and The Rev. John Evans (c. 1768 - 1813), who was born at Lydney, Gloucestershire, and lived in Bristol and Winterbourne from about 1806 - 1810. Our schoolmaster was born in the City of Bristol and educated, like G.W. Braikenridge ten years or so earlier, by the Reverend Dr. Estlin.

Described as a teacher of the classics, he kept for some years a "respectable boarding school" in Kingsdown. During part of this time (1816 - 20) he was also minister of the Presbyterian congregation at the Old Meeting House, Marshfield, and for a shorter period at the Grove Meeting, Bradford-on-Avon, where Presbyterians had adopted Unitarian views. Some time before his early death he moved to London, where he opened a classical day school near Euston Square.

In his Bristol years, John Evans must, on the evidence of his publications, have devoted a good deal of his time to local history of the more popular kind. Previously he had written a volume of essays, *The Ponderer*. William Tyson, in his unpublished historical collections for Bristol,[2] dismisses Evans as having done no more than "inflate" William Barrett's work, and refers to him as "an historian without research". However, his collaboration with John Corry in a history of the city seems to have been not unsuccessful, and each of them finds a niche in the *Dictionary of National Biography*.

Publications: *The Ponderer* (essays), 1812; *The Picture of Bristol, including biographical notices of Eminent Natives*, 1814; *Historical Account of the Church of St. Mary, Redcliffe*, 1815; *The History of Bristol*, Vol. II, 1816[3]; *Beauties of Clifton*, 1820.

MSS. None known.

Biographical sources: *D.N.B.*, *Gent. Mag.* cii, 372 - 3, 651; *The Christian Reformer*, Jan. - Dec., 1832, p.42; Jerom Murch, *A History of the Presbyterian and General Baptist Churches in the*

West of England, 1835, p.39 etc; C. Roy Hudleston, 'John Evans of Bristol', in *TBGAS*, xli (1939).

Notes.
1. Author of *A Chronological outline of the History of Bristol*, 1824; killed by the collapse of the Royal Brunswick Theatre in London, 29 Feb. 1828.
2. Vol. II, p.380 (in Central Library, Bristol). But see No. 29 (William Tyson) for Evans's part in the *Bristol Memorialist*.
3. Vol. I was written by John Corry, a London journalist.

27. George ORMEROD, 1785 - 1873

Ormerod's History of Cheshire, one of the standard county histories of the 19th century, is the work by which George Ormerod is chiefly known; in writing it he explored a vast accumulation of documents which he found in Chester Castle, as well as the Randle Holme collection for Cheshire in the British Museum. But he spent the latter part of his long life at Sedbury Park in Tidenham,[1] Gloucestershire, on the Beachley peninsula between Severn and Wye, where he studied and wrote on the history, archaeology and geology of the area.

Born in Manchester, he received his education at King's School, Chester and Brasenose, Oxford. A man of considerable intellectual powers and wide interests, he became a Fellow of the Society of Antiquaries in 1809, of the Royal Society in 1819, and of the Geological Society. Oxford University made him an honorary D.C.L. in 1818. His *Memoir on British and Roman Remains* [etc., in the Bristol Channel region] was read to the Archaeological Institute when it met at Bristol in 1851, and he contributed six papers to *Archaeologia*, but he produced no major work in later life. There is an engraving of his portrait, by John Jackson, R.A., in his Cheshire history.

Of Ormerod's ten children, no less than four joined him in the *Dictionary of National Biography*, — George Waring Ormerod as a geologist, William as a surgeon, Edward, F.R.S., as a physician and natural historian, and their sister Eleanor, a distinguished entomologist, who with her mother and sisters had provided the drawings for his archaeological papers. The eldest son, Thomas, was Archdeacon of Suffolk and an authority on Semitic languages.

Publications: History of the County Palatinate & City of Chester, 1819; papers on the archaeology and history of Cheshire and Lancashire; essays on the history and archaeology of the Forest of Dean area, Offa's Dyke, etc., including *Strigulensia,* 1861.

MSS. George Ormerod's notes and papers for a revised edition of his history of Cheshire, with his other manuscripts, including 9 volumes of Lancashire genealogical material, are (1979) in the possession of his descendant Mr. P.J. Ormerod of Maidstone. For Gloucestershire there are three volumes of notes, extracts and sketches, of which there are microfilm copies in the Gloucestershire Record Office, and a volume of pedigrees etc. of the medieval Ap Adam family of Beverstone, Glos. Elsewhere there are:

1. Bodleian Library, author's copy of the *History of the County Palatinate and City of Chester*, 1819, with extra-illustrations and additions.
2. Edinburgh Univ. Library (MS. Dept), 6 vols. of drawings by George Ormerod, his wife Sarah, and daughters G.E., S.M. and E.L. Ormerod. Of these, Vols. II and VI include Gloucestershire material.

Biographical sources: *D.N.B.*; *D.N.B., 2nd Suppt.* (Eleanor Ormerod): preface to 2nd edn. of Ormerod's *History ... of Chester;* (autobiography of) *Eleanor Ormerod*, 1904; *Proc. of Soc. of Antiquaries*, 2nd ser., vi, 196; *Athenaeum*, 18 Oct. 1873, p. 498; *Glos. N. & Q.*, 2, 462.

Note. 1. George Ormerod bought the estate in 1825 (see *V.C.H. Glos.*, x, 63).

28. James BENNETT, 1785 - 1856

In James Bennett we have a local man whose work, based largely on printed sources but sound enough within its limitations, was confined to the history of one very ancient and interesting town, Tewkesbury. He was born at Falfield in Gloucestershire, educated at 'Mr. Daw's school' at Stone near Berkeley, apprenticed in Bath, and employed as a printer, first in London, afterwards on the Gloucester Journal. The rest of his life, from 1810 to 1852, was spent as a printer and bookseller in Tewkesbury, of which borough, as well as of Gloucester, he was a freeman.

Bennett's *History of Tewkesbury*, though evidently much indebted to William Dyde's *History and Antiquities of Tewkesbury*, 1790 (to which Bennett failed to make any acknowledgement!) is more sophisticated, and has valuable appendices giving abstracts of borough records, etc. He supplemented the history for twenty years by his *Yearly Register*, which contains a number of historical papers as well as a record of current events. Both *History* and *Register*, of course, were printed by himself; the *Register*, he says in his preface, was undertaken chiefly for his own amusement.

Among other activities, James Bennett was director of the Tewkesbury public charities; he was also a churchwarden, and his obituary in the *Gentleman's Magazine* records that the fabric of Tewkesbury Abbey church owed much to his watchfulness and care.

Publications: *The History of Tewkesbury*, 1830 (reprinted 1976); *The Tewkesbury Yearly Register and Magazine*, 1830 - 49; *A Tewkesbury Guide*, 1835 and later (abbreviated from the *History*).

MSS. Bennett (preface to his *History*) refers to his "voluminous" collections, but no manuscript material has been traced.

Biographical sources: *D.N.B.*; *Gent. Mag.*, 1830, pt.1, 605 - 07 (review of the *History*), 1833, 146 (review of the *Yearly Register*), 1856, 317 - 18 (obit.); C.R. Elrington, F.S.A., Introduction to 1976 re-issue of the *History of Tewkesbury*.

29. William TYSON, 1785 - 1851

In the Bristol solicitor's office where William Tyson started his working life, he made the acquaintance of ancient deeds relating to city property, and these aroused an interest in the past which never waned. He collected books and bygones, and eventually, about 1820, opened a bookshop in Clare Street. About 1826, however, he gave this up to join the staff of the *Bristol Mirror* (later *Times & Mirror*), spending the rest of his days as a journalist and becoming editor of the paper.

As early as 1816 the lawyer's clerk had issued a prospectus for a quarterly magazine to be entitled *The Bristol Memorialist*, dealing with the antiquities and history of the city. Only four parts were issued, three in 1816 and one in 1823. Tyson's partner in this enterprise was the Rev. John Evans (No. 26), who in a letter of July 1828[1] says that the *Memorialist* was Tyson's idea and that the first three numbers were produced under their joint editorship, the fourth by Tyson alone. Evidently the joint compilers had to write most of the contributions themselves.[2] Not more than 250 copies of any issue were printed, and the complete volume is now very scarce.

Tyson produced no more books, though he must have contemplated writing a new history of Bristol; his memoranda and collections for this still exist (see below). For many years he wrote for his newspaper a regular column of notes on local history and biography, signed with a gothic T. He also contributed to the *Gentleman's Magazine* and other journals.

His repute as an authority on local history grew. In a testimonial for the Fellowship of the Society of Antiquaries, to which he was elected in 1830, the antiquary and topographer John Britton refers to Tyson as "a gentleman well versed in the history and antiquities of England, and particularly zealous and diligent in developing the antiquities of his native city."[3] His obituary in the *Gentleman's Magazine* calls him "a full and reliable chronicler, who but for diffidence would have become more than locally celebrated". He was made an honorary member of the Somerset Archaeological Society. Shortly before his death he read a paper to the Royal Archaeological Institute at its Meeting of 1851, the first held in Bristol, for which he also acted as local secretary.[4]

A portrait of Tyson by a local artist, H.S. Parkman, which was given in 1910 to the Bristol Museum and Art Gallery, shows him holding an old deed with seal.

Publications: (ed. and part author) *The Bristol Memorialist*, 1816 - 1823; articles in the *Bristol Mirror*; contributions to the *Gent. Mag.* and archaeological journals.

MSS. Bris. L., Jefferies Collection: collections for a history of Bristol (2 vols.); Bris. L. 23999: other memoranda; B.R.O., 08160(i): transcripts of Bristol parish records.

Biographical sources: obit. in *Gent. Mag.*, n.s. xxxvi (Dec. 1851), p.662; biog.notices in Bris. L., Jefferies Colln., Vol. I, f.1 and Vol. III; *Bristol Times & Mirror*, 20 Oct. 1910 (presentation of portrait), recollections of Tyson.

Notes.
1. Inserted in the Glos. Coll. copy of the *Bristol Memorialist* (see illustration 26).
2. Those signed W. or T. were by Tyson, while Evans signed his variously 'The Ponderer', 'Philander', 'Cleanthus', 'The Wanderer', and 'M'. Other contributors are also mentioned in the letter.
3. Appended by Britton to a letter from G.W. Braikenridge to Britton, 5 Jan. 1830 (Bris. L., B22992).
4. George Ormerod and the Rev. H.T. Ellacombe were among other local antiquaries who read papers.

30. Henry Thomas ELLACOMBE, 1790 - 1885

A son of a Devon parson, H.T. Ellacombe after taking his degree at Oxford, studied engineering — rather unusually, for that date — under M.I. Brunel at Chatham Dockyard, but in 1816 was ordained.He spent the next thirty-three years at Bitton in south Gloucestershire, as curate, 1817 - 35 and Vicar, 1835 - 50. At the age of sixty he returned to his native county of Devon as Rector of Clyst St. George, where he remained for the rest of his life; but he was buried at Bitton, where there is a memorial to him.

Besides his life-long interests in local history and in botany, Ellacombe (F.S.A., 1827) was well known as a campanologist and writer on church bells, and he invented an apparatus — thanks, no doubt, to his training as an engineer — enabling one man to chime a set of bells. His pamphlet *Practical remarks on belfries and ringers*, originally a paper read to the Bristol Architectural Society in 1849, proved so practical that it was reprinted four times by 1884.

Ellacombe, who changed the spelling of his name from Ellicombe, restored Bitton church in 1822 and built three other churches. His history of Bitton was produced at the age of 91, but a letter of 1823[1] shows that he was already intending to write it sixty years before. He was a contributor to *Notes & Queries* from its first issue (1849) until the year of his death.

Publications: *Practical remarks on belfries and ringers*, 1850; *History and Antiquities of the parish of Clyst St. George* [Devon], 1865; *Memoir of the Manor of Bitton*, 1869; *The Church Bells of Devon*, 1872; *The Church Bells of Somerset*, 1875; *The Church Bells of Gloucestershire*, 1881; *History of the Parish of Bitton*, 1881 - 3.

MSS. 1. B.L., Add. 33202-06. Collections and correspondence relating to church bells, 1824 - 1882, bequeathed to the British Museum. The B.L. MS. Dept. also has a few stray letters from Ellacombe.

2. Bristol Central Library, 7380 - 7396. Antiquarian notes, drawings, correspondence, transcripts, etc., with some collected MSS., mounted in 15 very large and 2 small vols. Much of this

collection relates to Gloucestershire and to Ellacombe's works on church bells. Vol. 6 contains a memorandum dated 1896, by John Latimer, the Bristol Librarian, on the Ellacombe bequest.

Ellacombe, by his will proved in 1885, left to "the Library Society in Bristol or to the Bristol Library, as my executors may think best" all his manuscripts, etc. relating to Bitton and Gloucestershire, except those relating to the Court Farm at Bitton. However, he had owned a considerable collection of original manuscripts, mostly relating to Gloucestershire, which were described in the Fifth Report of the Historical Manuscripts Commission (1876). At the end of Vol. 2 of the Ellacombe Papers in the Bristol Library (see above) there is a cutting of the H.M.C. Report, with a note by Ellacombe: "Many of these papers are now in the British Museum". In fact, Ellacombe sold to the Museum in 1879 the bulk of the records described in 1876, and they are now B.L. Add. Ch. 26417 - 513 and Add. MSS. 30939 G and 31123. These include medieval deeds of Bristol, 17th century papers relating to Kingswood Forest, and correspondence of the Newton family of Barr's Court concerning Monmouth's Rebellion.

3. The Bristol Record Office has a small collection (ref. 5139) of original local records which apparently belonged to Ellacombe and were formerly in the Bristol Museum.

4. The Gloucestershire Record Office has a group of papers of the Newton family (ref. D. 1844) which may also have been owned by Ellacombe but came from a depositor in Berkshire.

Biographical sources: *D.N.B.;* obituaries in *TBGAS*, ix, 365, *Glos. N. & Q.*, 3, 230-31, and *Church Bells*, 7 Aug. 1885; Thomas Mozley, *Reminiscences*, pp.75 - 81; [Canon] *Henry Nicholson Ellacombe, 1822 - 1916, A Memoir*, ed. A.W. Hill (pp. 11 - 31 concern H.T. Ellacombe, his father).

Notes. 1. From a member of the Creswick family to Ellacombe, in Bris. L. 7387.

31. Samuel Roffey MAITLAND, 1792 - 1866

A scholar, historian, archivist and writer of distinction, S.R. Maitland published nothing on Gloucestershire, but he was a Gloucestershire man and inherited from his mother the lordship of the manor of Brookthorpe, near Gloucester.

Originally Congregationalist, and so debarred at that time from taking a university degree, he studied at Trinity, Cambridge and was called to the Bar, but was received into the Church of England and ordained in 1821. He was incumbent of Christ Church, Gloucester for a few years from 1823,[1] but sought no preferment in the Church, and apart from travel abroad consecrated his life to historical research.

Having in 1832 published a learned monograph on the Albigensian and Waldensian heresies, and in 1835 some remarkable essays on the Dark Ages and on the Reformation, Maitland had achieved considerable standing as an ecclesiastical historian when, in 1838, he accepted the post of Librarian and Keeper of Manuscripts at Lambeth Palace,[2] which he held for the rest of his life, though he returned to live in retirement in Gloucester from 1849. An archiepiscopal D.D. was conferred on him in 1839 and from the same year until 1849 he was editor of the *British Magazine*. He became a Fellow of the Royal Society (1839) and of the Society of Antiquaries (1841), and was elected to the Council of the Antiquaries in 1844.

S.R. Maitland's interests were far from being confined to the subject of Church history. Described in the D.N.B. as musician, draughtsman, versed in both ancient and modern languages, and a brilliant conversationalist, he was the author of no less than thirty-seven works, some of them printed in Gloucester. He did not actually originate the famous antiquarian journal *Notes & Queries*, but to his encouragement and assistance the appearance of No. 1, on 3 November 1849, may mainly be attributed.[3] His contributions on many subjects to the early numbers were sometimes signed 'Rufus'. "In him .... learning the most deep and varied was intermingled with extraordinary wit and humour".[3] His repute has perhaps been overshadowed by that of another Gloucestershire celebrity, his grandson Frederick William Maitland, the greatest English constitutional historian.

Publications: S.R. Maitland's many works, mainly historical and theological, appear to include nothing on local history, but see below under *MSS*. F.W. Maitland, whose papers were published in three volumes (ed. H.A.L. Fisher) in 1911, edited (1894) *Pleas of the Crown for the County of Gloucester in the year 1221.*

MSS. 1. Glos. Coll., 2091. List of works of Bishops, Deans, etc. of Gloucester, with biographical notes. (51 pp.)
   2. Glos. Coll., 13593. Biographical notes on Miles Smith, Bishop of Gloucester (33 pp.)
   3. Cambridge Univ. Library. A copy of Strype's works on Church history, collated by Maitland in MS. with the original sources in books and MSS. at Lambeth.
   4. Lambeth Palace Library, MSS. 1943 - 45. 36 letters of Maitland's and two vols. of sketches relating to a Continental tour in 1828.

There seems to be no large group of Maitland's manuscripts, unless perhaps with his descendants. According to the *D.N.B.*, he left an autobiography of his early years, up to 1817 only.

Biographical sources: *D.N.B.* ; *Gent. Mag.*, 1866 (i), 590 - 1; *N. & Q.*, ser. 3, ix, 90 (obituary), ser. 5, x, 326 - 7; *Proc., Royal Society*, xvi, p. xxi.

Notes. 1. A letter from W.E. Gladstone, 1880, printed in *Glos. N. & Q.*, 4, 318, on his recollections of Gloucester in 1825, mentions "a dry but learned and able clergyman named Maitland".
   2. "When invited to take the office of librarian at Lambeth", writes a contributor to *N. & Q.* (ser. 4, i, 50), "he was living in his own house at Gloucester. He gave up that, took a house in Town at £200 a year, paid a clerk to assist him at 2 guineas a week, and received in return the enormous salary of £40 a year."
   3. Obituary in *N. & Q.*

32. Sir Thomas PHILLIPPS, Bt., 1792 - 1872

In his five volumes of 'Phillipps Studies' (see below), the late A.N.L. Munby has left us a masterly and comprehensive account of the Phillipps Collection and its personally not very edifying owner, the 'vellomaniac'. Thomas Phillipps, probably the greatest manuscript collector of all time, was not quite a Gloucestershire man, but he had strong links with the county, and ended his days at Thirlestane House in Cheltenham.

He was the bastard but acknowledged son of a rich cotton manufacturer, Thomas Phillipps, who had bought the estate of Middle Hill in Broadway, on the Gloucestershire border, and the manors of Buckland and Laverton in Gloucestershire. His son was sent to Rugby and Oxford, and having succeeded to the property on his father's death in 1818, contrived to get himself created a baronet in 1821, in the Coronation honours of George IV. From an early age he had displayed a passion for collecting books and manuscripts, and had in 1819 become a Fellow of the Society of Antiquaries, to whose Council he was eventually elected forty years later. The suppression of religious houses in France by the Revolution, and the dispersal of their libraries, had given opportunities for the collector only comparable to those of the Reformation era in England, but Phillipps also bought widely and continuously in his own country.

About 1822 Sir Thomas set up a private press at his home, Middle Hill, where he printed many records, genealogies, catalogues of manuscripts, etc., including later on the 'Continuations' of Bigland's *History of Gloucestershire*. The collections and memoranda of other Gloucestershire antiquaries, in particular T.D. Fosbroke, were likewise among those which passed into his hands. In 1864 Phillipps, whose collecting mania had involved him, despite his large inheritance, in financial difficulties, leased Thirlestane House in Cheltenham from Lord Northwick for his by then vast collection. He died there eight years later. Since 1886 the collection has been gradually dispersed, mainly at auction. In 1945 the residue, still in crates in the cellars of Thirlestane House, was acquired by the booksellers Lionel and Philip Robinson, and recently, after further large sales, a final residue has passed to

M.P. Kraus of New York. Phillipps's own correspondence and papers, with odds and ends of his collection, are now in the Bodleian Library (MSS. Phillipps-Robinson).

Sir William Guise, in his presidential address to the first annual meeting of the Bristol and Gloucestershire Archaeological Society, mentioned that Sir Thomas Phillipps had bestowed time and pains in arranging and binding the earlier Wills in the Gloucester probate registry. He was a member of the first Record Commission, and protested against its termination.

The personal relationships of this eccentric, including his efforts to arrange his daughters' marriages to his financial advantage, and his feuds with his son-in-law the Shakespearian scholar J.O. Halliwell (afterwards Halliwell-Phillipps) and others, are entertainingly related in Volume II of Munby's *Phillipps Studies*. There are good photographs of Phillipps, in 1834 and 1860, in Volumes III and IV respectively. Munby also published in facsimile Phillipps's own Catalogue, giving details of his purchases and showing where many of them were made. Messrs. Sotheby have an annotated copy of this, from which the sale dates of Phillipps items sold by them can be traced, and sometimes the purchasers.

Publications: Practically nothing original. Phillipps edited *Visitations of Gloucestershire, 1569, etc* and *1684* among many other Heralds' Visitations, besides parts of the Bigland 'Continuations'. A paper on the Flaxley Abbey cartulary, read by him in 1827, is printed in the *Transactions of the Royal Society of Literature*, i, 53 - 56. For a list of Gloucestershire material printed by Phillipps at the Middle Hill press, see *Glos. N. & Q.*, 4, 394.

MSS. Bodl., MSS. Phillipps-Robinson, correspondence and papers of Sir Thos. Phillipps, with some original records from the Phillipps Collection. Such other material as he has left consists mainly in transcripts. (see Munby, *Phillipps Studies,* II, 101). Phillipps's will directed that his printing presses etc. should be used in finishing incomplete work and in printing his 'inedited historical works, some being unique'. Sir Frederick Madden (Keeper of Manuscripts, British Museum) commented: .... "if the whole were put in the fire it would be no loss whatever".

Biographical sources: *D.N.B.*; *Athenaeum*, 10 Feb. 1872, obit. by J.O. Halliwell-Phillipps; A.N.L. Munby, *Phillipps Studies* (5 vols), 1951 - 60, viz. I, *The Catalogues of MSS. and Printed Books of Sir Thomas Phillipps;* II, *The Family Affairs of Sir Thomas Phillipps;*

III, *The Foundation of the Phillipps Library up to the year 1840*, and IV, *between 1841 and 1872*; V, *The Dispersal of the Phillipps Library*.

33. John Daniel Thomas NIBLETT, 1809 - 1883

Unknown to fame outside his own county, this Gloucestershire landowner, Justice of the Peace, and amateur historian played some part in the 19th century expansion of local studies. The family had risen to prosperity as bakers in Gloucester,[1] but J.D.T. Niblett inherited Haresfield Court from his father Daniel John Niblett, who had been High Sheriff of the county in 1816.

J.D.T. Niblett, a collector of Gloucestershire books,[2] became a member of the Cotteswold Naturalists' Field Club, which was established in 1846 and absorbed a short-lived Gloucestershire Archaeological Society, whose honorary secretary he had been. Thirty years later he joined the 'B. & G.' on its foundation. He was also a member of a committee for restoring the celebrated Fairford church windows, and a letter of 1845 shows that he intended to write a detailed description of them for publication. At one time, according to his obituary notice in the *Transactions* of the Bristol & Gloucestershire Society, he "contemplated, in association with the late Mr. John Jones of Gloucester,[3] the compilation of a new history of the county, and had made considerable collections for the purpose, but from some cause the design was never carried out." In the end, like other well-intentioned local historians, he published nothing; but his notebooks, now in the Gloucester Library, are of some interest. He was an Oxford graduate and was elected an F.S.A. in 1863.

Publications: none.

MSS. 1. Glos. Coll., 1: Commonplace books, 1834 - c.1870 including antiquarian notes (2 vols.).
2. Glos. Coll., 3490 and 12094: Heraldic note-books.
3. Glos. Coll., 8627: Notes and correspondence on Fairford church glass, 1845 - 69..

Biographical sources: *TBGAS*, viii, 243 (obit.); *Records of Gloucester Cathedral*, Vol. 2, 172-3 (obit.).

Notes. 1. Deeds in G.R.O., D 878.
        2. The Gloucestershire portion of his library was sold on 18 Sept. 1884. (Catalogue in Glos. Coll., 2121.)

3. A member of the C.N.F.C., and secretary of the Gloucester Literary and Scientific Institution, who seems to have been chiefly a geologist, but the Glos. Coll. (12082) has a book of Gloucestershire pedigrees, etc., with heraldic drawings, and the Bodleian Library (MSS. Phillipps-Robinson, d.49) a portfolio of 55 drawings of church monuments etc., both his work.

34. Sir John MACLEAN, 1811 - 1895

Born at Blisland in Cornwall but presumably of Highland ancestry, John, son of Robert Lean, changed his name back to Maclean in 1845. His working life was spent as a civil servant, employed in the War Office and rising to be Deputy Chief Auditor of Army Accounts, where his services brought him a knighthood in 1871. Retiring in the same year to the West Country, he lived first near Coleford in the Forest of Dean, and from about 1887 at Clifton.

Maclean had become a Fellow of the Society of Antiquaries in 1855 and later served on their Council, besides being a Vice-President of the Royal Archaeological Institute. He was a founder member of the Harleian Society in 1869, and edited two volumes for the Camden Society. Though his historical and archaeological activities had been principally in his native Cornwall, Gloucestershire soon shared them to the full, and he was one of the most zealous of the enthusiasts who formed the Bristol & Gloucestershire Archaeological Society in 1876. For many years he was an enterprising and influential member. Despite his age, he directed the Tockington Roman Villa excavation, and was editor of the Society's *Transactions* from 1878 to 1894, himself contributing over fifty papers, for the most part on archival subjects of value for the history of the county. Sir John was President of the Society in 1881, having already been President of the Royal Institution of Cornwall, to whose *Journal* he was likewise a frequent contributor, as well as to *Notes & Queries*.

Publications: *Life of Sir Thomas Seymour, Lord Seymour of Sudeley*, 1869; *Annals of Chepstow Castle*, 1883; ed. *The Berkeley Manuscripts (Lives of the Berkeleys* and *The Hundred of Berkeley)* by John Smith of Nibley (see No. 3), 1883-5; *Memoir of the Family of Poyntz*, 1886; co-editor of the Harleian Society's *Visitation of Gloucestershire* (1623), 1885, and *Visitation of Cornwall* (1620), 1874; *History of the Deanery of Trigg Minor* (Cornwall), 1868-79.

MSS. Royal Inst. of Cornwall, Maclean MSS. in Brooks Collection. These relate entirely to Cornwall; no manuscript papers of Maclean concerning Gloucestershire have been located.

Biographical sources: *D.N.B.*; obit. in *TBGAS*, xix, 168-9; *Bibliotheca Cornubiensis*, i, 333-4 and iii, 1273.

35. Thomas KERSLAKE, 1812 - 1891

Like William Tyson before him, and William George a little later, Thomas Kerslake was a Bristol bookseller. He and George between them gained the city a reputation as a centre for antiquarian books. Kerslake was in business from about 1828 to 1870, and his catalogues were "curiosities of learning". Unluckily much of his fine collection of books was destroyed by fire in 1860. After retirement he devoted himself to historical research and controversy. He was one of the founders of the Clifton Antiquarian Club, and although self-taught he achieved some distinction as an antiquary. In the words of the *D.N.B.*, his writings were marked by shrewdness and originality. William George, in his memoir (see below), described Kerslake, whom he knew well, as "a man of intrepid self-reliance, strong character, and somewhat defiant temper", who "pursued his enquiries ... with the patience and diligence of an early Schoolman." His particular fields were pre-history and the Anglo-Saxon period in south-west England; his published work, not inconsiderable, was usually in the form of essays, printed at his own expense. He died at Clevedon, Somerset.

Publications: for full list, see index to the *Catalogue of the Somerset Archaeological Society's Library*, Taunton, 1889. Kerslake also made frequent contributions to local newspapers.

MSS: Nothing is known of any manuscript material.

Biographical sources: *D.N.B.*; *Biog. Suppt.*, I, 264-5; *Athenaeum*, I, 53-4, 'Mr. Kerslake'; *Somerset Archaeological & Natural History Society, Proceedings*, Vol. 37 (1891), 131-3: 'In Memoriam, Thomas Kerslake', by William George; *Clifton Antiquarian Club, Proceedings*, Vol. II, 273-4.

36. John GODING, 1816 - 1879

When John Goding, who was born at Marylebone in London,[1] was a boy of about twelve, his parents moved to the spa of Cheltenham, then growing at a prodigious rate. They kept a grocer's shop, which their son later carried on. He joined a group of men who held religious meetings and eventually built the Unitarian church in Cheltenham; he was also active as a Radical in local politics. His zeal for Unitarianism led him to investigate its history in Cheltenham, which went back to about 1700 but had lapsed for half a century.

Goding's interest in Cheltenham history grew, and in his leisure time he "devoted himself with untiring perseverance and industry to .... local antiquities .... No walk was too long, no labour too great, in the pursuit of his favourite employment."[2] His *History of Cheltenham* (1853) had previously come out in weekly instalments in the *Cheltenham Free Press*. Largely self-educated, and with comparatively little spare time, he thus produced the first serious attempt at a full historical account of the town, earlier 'histories' of which had been more in the nature of guide books. Mrs. Hart, in her recent and much more sophisticated *History of Cheltenham*, says of Goding that although he was untrained (and sometimes unreliable), he was the only writer of his generation who realized the importance of the sources then available. Certainly he put to shame many leisured or retired residents of the spa who must have been better equipped to tackle the task.

From about 1860 to 1870 John Goding wrote regular articles on local history for the *Cheltenham Examiner*. From 1865 he was Assistant Overseer of the Poor and rate collector for the populous parish, which did not achieve the status of a municipal borough until 1876. "Such was his benevolent disposition", according to a memoir in the Unitarian journal *The Christian Life*, "that in spite of his religious and political convictions, and the uncompromising way in which he asserted them, he was on the best of terms with fellow-townsmen of all shades of opinion."

Publications: *A History of Cheltenham, from the earliest period to the present time*, 1853, revised and enlarged by the author as *Norman's History of Cheltenham*, 1863[3]; papers in the *Cheltenham Examiner*, c. 1860 - 70.

MSS. No surviving historical material has been traced, except for a brief 'History of the [Unitarian] Society', prefixed to the Register of the Transactions of Public Meetings of the Unitarian Congregation at Cheltenham, 1844 - 78. The earlier part of the Register, which is among the records of the Congregation, is in John Goding's handwriting, as secretary from 1839 to 1849.

Biographical sources: obituary in *Cheltenham Examiner*, 30 Apr. 1879; memoir in *The Christian Life*, 6 May 1899; Gwen Hart, *A History of Cheltenham* (1965), Preface, vii - viii; information from Cheltenham Library.

Notes.
1. Cheltenham census return, 1861.
2. *Cheltenham Examiner*, 30 Apr. 1879.
3. G. Norman, of the *Cheltenham Examiner*, was the publisher.

37. David ROYCE, 1817 - 1902

The Reverend David Royce, Vicar of the Cotswold parish of Nether Swell for fifty-two years (1850 - 1902), was offered other livings including the important one of Cirencester, but declined them, preferring to give a large share of his time to historical research and archaeology.

A son of Matthew Royce of Oakham in Rutland, he was born there and educated at Oakham Grammar School before taking a degree from Christ Church, Oxford, returning to his college as chaplain for some years after ordination. He maintained his Oxford connections as joint General Secretary from 1872 and Vice-President from 1890 of the N. Oxfordshire Archaeological Socy., of which he had been a founder-member in 1853. In 1876 he also joined the Bristol & Gloucestershire Society on its foundation, becoming a member of its Council in 1883, and a Vice-President in 1894.

This self-effacing scholar made valuable collections of pre-historic flint implements, fossils, coins and trade tokens, now in the Bristol Museum. He assisted in some local excavations in the Stow-on-the-Wold neighbourhood. After other useful contributions to North Gloucestershire history, all his leisure during his last twenty years was consecrated to editing the great 13 - 15 cent. cartulary or 'landboc' of Winchcombe Abbey; he died before finishing the Introduction to Volume II. His valuable library of archaeological books was given by his widow to the B.G.A.S.

Publications: *The History & Antiquities of Stow*[-on-the-Wold], 1861; *Icomb: its History, Topography and Architectural Antiquities* (a paper read to the Worcester Diocesan Architectural Society), 1869; *History of the Church of Bourton-on-the-Water*, 1874; (ed.) *Landboc sive Registrum monasterii .... de Winchelcumba ....*, 1892, 1903; papers in *TBGAS* and *Trans. of N. Oxfordshire Archaeological Socy.*

MSS. 1. Many papers in BGAS Library (Gloucester Ref. Library), nearly all transcripts of records or extracts from county and other historians.
    2. B.L., Add. 33206, ff. 222-3; two letters to the Rev. H.T. Ellacombe (No. 30), 1871.

Biographical sources: Memorial preface, by Canon William Bazeley, to Vol. II of the *Winchcombe Landboc*, 1903; memoir by Bazeley in *A Catalogue of Books from the Library of the late Rev. D. Royce*, 1903; L.V. Grinsell, 'The Royce Collection at Stow-on-the-Wold', in *TBGAS*, lxxxiii, 5-33, with Supplement in *TBGAS*, lxxxv, 209-213.

38. Beaver Henry BLACKER, 1821 - 1890

An Irish clergyman, the Rev. B.H. Blacker, who had been born in Dublin and educated at Trinity College,[1] spent his first fifty years and more in Ireland, and was Rural Dean of South Dublin from 1862 to 1874. Migrating to Gloucestershire, he held curacies at Charlton Kings and Cheltenham from 1875 to 1878, living afterwards for a time in Stroud and from 1881 in Clifton. His later years seem to have been devoted entirely to historical research, and he is said to have contributed more than sixty articles to the *Dictionary of National Biography*. His contributions to *Notes & Queries*, signed *ABHBA*, extended from 1853 to 1890. He also collected material for a bibliography of Gloucestershire.

In 1878 Blacker started — in the Stroud Journal — *Gloucestershire Notes & Queries*, which he edited until his death and which went on until 1914, though in its last years spasmodically. It is today a mine of useful information, — *si monumentum requiris, circumspice*. Many of the best Notes are his own. W.P.W. Phillimore, writing Blacker's obituary, said: "The name of this unassuming student will be, as it deserves, long remembered for the substantial service which for fifteen years he did in the by-paths of Gloucestershire history". William George of Bristol called him a zealous, cautious and painstaking antiquary, and one who felt as much pleasure in communicating as in gathering information.

There is a photograph of Blacker in Vol. 5 of *Glos. N. & Q.*

Publications: *Brief sketches of the parishes of Bootersdown and Donnybrook, Co. Dublin*, 1860 - 74; *Monumental Inscriptions in the Parish Church of Charlton Kings*, 1876, and *of Cheltenham*, 1877; contributions to the *D.N.B.* and periodicals (see above).

MSS. Nothing has been traced, except an incomplete catalogue of his library, now Glos. Coll. 12412.

Biographical sources: *Glos. N. & Q.*, 5, 1-4 (obituary notices); *Proc. Clifton Antiquarian Club*, II, 273.

Note. 1. The *Alumni Dublinenses* gives him as son of Latham Blacker, solicitor, and the date of his M.A. degree as 1846.

39. Henry George NICHOLLS, 1822 - 1867

In recent years Dr. Cyril Hart has produced a series of monographs on different aspects of the Forest of Dean and its history, shedding much light on that beautiful and rather mysterious region, where descendants of the warlike Silures mingle with those of 18th century squatters on the Crown lands. The Forest has had one earlier historian, a century before, — an Anglican clergyman who died at the age of forty-four after writing three short books in the course of a brief and strenuous life.

The Rev. H.G. Nicholls was the only son of a remarkable reformer and administrator, Sir George Nicholls, K.C.B. (1781 - 1865), who lived for a time at Longford, near Gloucester. After service at sea, George Nicholls started the first savings bank, and instituted effective reforms in poor relief. A friend of Robert Peel and of Thomas Telford the engineer, he collaborated with Telford in canal enterprises, and in 1823 took charge of the Gloucester-Berkeley canal, reviving its failing fortunes. He also wrote extensively on poor relief, having become one of the three commissioners under the New Poor Law of 1834, and in 1847 permanent secretary of the Poor Law Board.

It is not surprising that the son of such a man, after Rugby (under Arnold) and Trinity, Cambridge, should have chosen in 1847 the newly created parish of Holy Trinity, Drybrook, in the heart of Dean Forest. In the early 19th century much of the Forest had been still extra-parochial, a wilderness lacking churches and schools, poverty-stricken and scarcely civilized.[1] H.G. Nicholls, described as "a man of immense energy and capability for hard work",[2] played a leading part for twenty years in fostering religious life and the building of schools in this depressed area. He resigned his living in 1866 through ill-health and died the following year, but in 1858 had published the first and only general history of the Forest of Dean, following it up in 1863 and 1866 with two other books, on Forest personalities and on the ancient iron industry of Dean.

Publications: *The Forest of Dean; an historical and descriptive account ....*, 1858; *The Personalities of the Forest of Dean*, 1863;

Iron-making in the olden times, as instanced in the ancient mines, forges, and furnaces of the Forest of Dean ...., 1866; 'The ancient iron trade in the Forest of Dean', in the *Archaeological Journal*, xvii (1860) 227-239. The first two books were reissued in one volume, with an index, by Dr. Cyril Hart, 1966.

MSS. Nothing is known of Nicholls's manuscripts, except that Dr. Cyril Hart, of Coleford, has a draft title-page, preface and contents of the *Personalities of the Forest of Dean*, with a letter from Nicholls and letters to him from the mining engineer Thomas Sopwith and others. In the Public Records Office, F3/209, there are several letters from Nicholls to the Office of Works (as responsible for Crown Forests) in a file of the 1860s concerning the parochial school of Holy Trinity, Drybrook.

Biographical sources: *D.N.B.* (article on Sir George Nicholls); Dr. Cyril Hart, *Introduction* to centenary reissue of the Rev. H.G. Nicholls's works, 1966.

Notes. 1. See Reports of the Commissioners for the Forest of Dean, 1835.
2. Cyril Hart, Introduction to reissue, 1966 (see *Publications*).

40. John LATIMER, 1824 - 1904

The birthplace of John Latimer was Newcastle-upon-Tyne, where he was educated at a private school and became a journalist. Migrating to Bristol in 1858, he edited the Bristol Mercury for twenty-five years.

Latimer had begun to keep a diary at the age of twelve, and his *Local Records* (see below) are a chronicle of events in Northumberland and Durham from 1832 to 1857. A "born annalist", gifted with great accuracy and industry, he spent most of his later life in documentary research on Bristol, working backwards from the nineteenth to the sixteenth century, with copious results, some published posthumously. He was a Vice-President of the Clifton Antiquarian Club, joined the Bristol & Gloucestershire Archaeological Society on its foundation, and was a member of its Council and honorary secretary for Bristol from 1894 to 1900. He is said to have received much encouragement in his writing from his somewhat younger contemporary F.F. Fox (No. 44).

Publications: Local Records of Northumberland and Durham, 1857. The Annals of Bristol in the Nineteenth Century, 1887, Eighteenth Century, 1893, and Seventeenth Century, 1900; History of the Merchant Venturers of Bristol, 1903; Sixteenth Century Bristol, 1908; Calendar of the Charters etc. of the County & City of Bristol, 1909; numerous contributions to *TBGAS* and *Proc. Clifton Ant. Club.*

MSS. 1. Bris. L., interleaved copy of Barrett's *History of Bristol*, with annotations by John Latimer.

2. B.R.O., Calendar of the Ellacombe MSS. and other material, compiled by Latimer 1894.

Latimer's own drafts and Memoranda, if any exist, have not been located.

Biographical sources: *TBGAS*, xxvi, 208-12 (obit. with portrait); *Proc. Clifton Ant. Club.* Vol. V, 277-8 (with frontispiece portrait); *Biog. Suppl.*, I, 270.

41. John Randall CLARKE, 1827 or 1828 - 1863

J.R. Clarke, who published an architectural history of Gloucester City in his early twenties, died at the age of thirty-six. The brief notice in the *Dictionary of National Biography*, derived partly from private information, tells us that he adopted architecture as his profession but devoted more of his time to literature. A little more can be gleaned from the *Gentleman's Magazine*, to which he contributed a number of articles.

He was the son of Joseph Clarke, Inspector of Stamps and Taxes for Gloucestershire and Wiltshire, who was a member of the Gloucester Literary and Scientific Association and one of the committee responsible for organizing the opening of their museum to the public in 1860; this became the Gloucester City Museum. Joseph Clarke was living at 4 College Green in 1863, when his son died there, but when he joined the Association in 1843 had an address in London Road; and F.W. Clarke, of the same address, had been a founding member in 1838.[1]

Had he lived a little later, or longer, John Randall Clarke might well have become — like John Bellows, born only a few years after — an active archaeologist. In his architectural history of 1850 he drew attention to Kingsholm and "the discoveries which marked this spot as a place of [Roman] sepulture". Shortly afterwards the excavations for a sewerage system in Gloucester brought to light Romano-British finds which aroused his enthusiasm and on which he sent a series of reports to the *Gentleman's Magazine* in 1853-55, with some of his own etchings of pottery etc. He lent Roman material found at Gloucester and Kingsholm to the temporary museum formed at Gloucester for the meeting of the Archaeological Institute there in 1860.[1]

There was little public interest in such things, and the young architect's letters to J.G. Nichols, editor of the Magazine,[2] express his feelings frankly. On 11th April 1854 he writes:

" .... in regard to what might be found, nobody looks after it but myself"

and on 17th April:

"I am so rejoiced to find that old Gloucester is at last beginning to show up as a mine of antiquities. By the way, these pursuits are apt to get me into trouble. I have been told several times that if our Corporation (sapient body!) see me poking so much about their works they will look upon me as a suspicious character, — the fact is they have stuck up a notice forbidding the abstraction of coins, and the consequence is the men throw all they find away. I am sure our aldermen expect to find some large 'pots of money'. As for the vases, etc., they treat them with utter contempt."

In the *Gentleman's Magazine* for September 1854 he comments more discreetly:

"One would imagine that some public interest would be excited at the discovery of these interesting relics, ... that corporate bodies or local institutions would gladly avail themselves of the opportunity of forming the nucleus of a local museum .... Alas! we relate with shame that no such interest was excited .... The tessalated pavement in Longsmith Street is an instance of Gloucester antiquarian zeal. Before Mr. Disney[3] could interfere, before a drawing could be made, or a note taken, a great part of the elaborate border had been broken with a pickaxe and sold bit by bit ...."

Clarke also published two historical romances and (like G.W. Counsel thirty years earlier) some facetious verses on local government in Gloucester, etc. Some of his frequent lectures to the Gloucester Literary and Scientific Association, including one on the churches of Gloucester, were apparently printed locally by subscription.

Publications: *The Architectural History of Gloucester, from the earliest period to the close of the eighteenth century*, 1850; *A popular account of the interesting priory of Llanthony, near Gloucester, etc.*, 1853.

MSS. None is known.

Biographical sources: *D.N.B.*; obituary (brief) in *Gent. Mag.*, 1863 (i), 671; *Cooper's Biog. Dict.*; *Gloucester Chronicle*, 4 Apr. 1863; *Gloucester Journal*, 4 Apr. and 3 Oct., 1863.

Notes: 1. Information kindly provided by Mr. J.F. Rhodes, Curator, Gloucester City Museum.
2. Four letters (1 May 1853 and 3, 11 and 17 Apr., 1854) now in the Fitzwilliam Museum, Cambridge, ref. L 55-58.
3. "the intelligent clerk of the works", who had been very cooperative.

42. John TAYLOR, 1829 - 1893

A lifelong citizen of Bristol, John Taylor was the son of another John, an ironmonger, and was born at Clifton. His education was at private schools, where he showed some mathematical ability and had a notion of being an engineer. However, things turned out quite otherwise. Having read widely and taught himself Latin and Greek in early manhood, he was in 1860 appointed Under-Librarian of the Bristol Library Society, and in 1863 its Librarian. The number of subscribers, which had been in decline, steadily increased, and ten years before his death he became City Librarian, from about seventy applicants.

Deeply interested in the history and antiquities of Bristol, Taylor, who had been a founder-member of the Clifton Antiquarian Club, read a paper on the subject to the British Archaeological Association at their meeting of 1874, held in the city; and this largely inspired the establishment in 1876 of the Bristol & Gloucestershire Archaeological Society, of whose Council he was an original member. Indeed, in 1887 he claimed to have been virtually its founder. As may be judged from the list of his published work below, John Taylor contributed extensively to local history.

Publications: *A Book about Bristol*, 1872; *Bristol and Clifton, Old and New*, 1878; *Bristol past and present*, Vol. 2, 1881; article on Bristol for the *Encyclopaedia Britannica*, 9th edn.; *Antiquarian Essays contributed to the Saturday Review*, 1895; papers in the *TBGAS*, *Proc. Clifton Ant. Club*, and other journals; etc.

MSS. Bris. L.: B 4836, 'Municipal constitutions of Bristol'; B.23796 note of references to Guilder's Inn and Hobson family, in 17th cent.; B.23798, notes on Canynge's Place, Redcliffe Hill. B.22426 is a vol. of letters written mainly *to* John Taylor.

Biographical sources:*D.N.B.*; *TBGAS*, obit. in vol. xvii and note in xviii, 7; obit. in *Proc. Clifton Ant. Club*, II, 273; memoir by William George, with portrait, in *Antiquarian Essays* (see above), 1895.

43. William GEORGE, 1830 - 1900

William George, of the well-known firm of Bristol booksellers which still bears his name, was born at Dunster in Somerset. His father died when he was only six years old, and at the age of twelve the boy was sent to work for a maternal uncle, William Strong, in Clare Street, Bristol, and to learn his business of bookselling and publishing. From a note by him (concerning his uncle's estate) dated 1877,[1] he appears to have been apprenticed either by the parish or by benevolence of the Luttrell family of Dunster Castle. The life was hard; he writes:– "W.S. should have taught me his trade, but up to his death I had to clean knives and forks, help to clean windows, and was only occasionally in the shop." His uncle, whose business had in fact been crippled by the burning of his premises in the Bristol riots of 1831, died in 1846, when young William George was sixteen.

The following year, having scraped together a capital of £50, he set up for himself as a bookseller. His first account book, which is still extant in the firm's archives, is written in a fine copperplate hand, and French exercises at the end of the book show how he was improving his education. In 1848 he issued his first catalogue, after which the business grew steadily.

George, who developed an interest in manuscripts as well as in printed books, left at his death a vast store of valuable MS. material. He had become a prominent citizen of Bristol, and a "keen and indefatigable student of the history and bibliography of Bristol and the adjoining counties". One of the founders of the Bristol & Gloucestershire Archaeological Society, he contributed occasionally to its *Transactions*, to other learned journals, and in later life to the *Dictionary of National Biography*; also to the *Bristol Times and Mirror* under the pseudonym 'Cabot'.

Publications: *Some account of the oldest plans of Bristol*, 1881. Otherwise only articles in periodicals.

MSS. Nothing of an antiquarian nature is known to have been preserved.

Biographical sources: Obituary in *TBGAS*, xxii, 302-03; *William George's Sons Ltd., Booksellers for a century*, 1947, foreword.

Note. 1. See Illustration 43.

44. Francis Frederick FOX, 1833 - 1915

F.F. Fox was a son of F.K. Fox, M.D., of Brislington, Somerset, now a suburb of Bristol. Educated at Shrewsbury, he established in early life a firm of oil and colour merchants, and was prominent in local government, serving as a J.P. for both Bristol and Gloucestershire, as an alderman of Bristol from 1865 and eventually senior alderman, as City Sheriff in 1880, and as Master of the Society of Merchant Venturers.

His spare-time predilections tended more towards collecting than writing, but he produced a book and a number of papers on the history of the Bristol and Sodbury areas, his home being latterly at Yate House near Chipping Sodbury. He was also an enthusiastic member of the Bristol and Gloucestershire Archaeological Society from the time of its foundation, President in 1900, and Chairman of Council from 1903 to 1908. His 'In Memoriam' notice in the Society's *Transactions* testifies to his "ability, geniality, and unvarying courtesy", and his fine library was at the service of enquirers. He became an F.S.A. in 1902, and in 1910 he published, at his own expense, the 17th century Bristol chronicle of William Adams (see No. 4), one manuscript of which he owned.

A great many local records and antiquarian miscellanea collected by F.F. Fox are now in the Bristol Record Office.

Publications: *History of the parishes of Old Sodbury and Chipping Sodbury and the Town of Chipping Sodbury*, 1907; articles in *TBGAS* on the Bristol and Sodbury gilds and other subjects.

MSS. B.R.O., 08153-60: original records, transcripts and memoranda, formerly owned by F.F. Fox (10 vols.). Some of these had been bought by the Rev. William Maskell (antiquary and ecclesiastical controversialist; see *D.N.B.*) at the sale of the effects of William Tyson, F.S.A. (No. 29) in 1851. They include: 08160 (1), transcripts of parish records by Tyson; and 08158, memoranda book of John White (b. at Devizes 1711) relating to Bristol.

Biographical sources: obituaries in *TBGAS*, xxvii, 247 - 9, and *Bristol Times & Mirror*, 5 June 1915; *Kelly's Handbook*, 1912.

45. William BAZELEY, 1843 - 1925

Although a Cornishman by birth (his father was nine times Mayor of St. Ives), William Bazeley, after taking a Cambridge degree and holy orders, spent all the rest of his life in Gloucestershire, being Rector of Matson near Gloucester for almost fifty years. He acted as secretary of the Gloucester Diocesan Conference from 1892 to 1907, and was promoter of the Gloucester Cathedral Society, and was made an honorary Canon of Gloucester in 1907.

A founder-member of the Bristol & Gloucestershire Archaeological Society, he was its honorary secretary, at first jointly, from 1879 to 1907, Chairman of Council 1908 - 1917, President for 1908 - 09, and a regular contributor to its *Transactions* from volume ii (1877) to volume xlvi (1924). He also read papers to the Society of Antiquaries, though rather surprisingly he never became a Fellow. His work for county bibliography and for the history of Gloucester Cathedral is of permanent value.

Canon Bazeley was indeed the life and soul of the Bristol & Gloucestershire Society in the first forty years of its existence, and was recognized as such. With his very intimate knowledge of Gloucestershire history, he frequently acted as guide for field meetings and for many years compiled elaborate meeting programmes with archaeological notes. On his death, Roland Austin wrote of his striking presence and unfailing good humour, adding that the work of the Society was one of the chief pleasures of his life. The 'B. & G.' had presented him with his portrait on his retirement from the secretaryship.

Publications: *Records of Gloucester Cathedral* (as editor and contributor), 1882 - 97; *A History of Prinknash Park*, 1890; *Notes on the Tudor carvings .... in 163 Westgate Street, Gloucester*, 1893; *The Bibliographer's Manual of Gloucestershire Literature* (in collaboration with F.A. Hyett), 1895 - 97; *A Catalogue of Books .... of the late Rev. D. Royce, with a memoir*, 1903; many papers in *TBGAS*, *Proc. C.N.F.C.*, etc.

MSS. 1. Glos. Coll., 6. Note-books (12 vols.), with a number of heraldic and other drawings (pages numbered through the whole series).

2. Glos. Coll., 9503-9505 and 9515. Memoranda and transcripts relating to Matson parish and the Selwyn family.

Biographical sources: Obituary (by Roland Austin) in *TBGAS*, xlvii, 380-84; Elizabeth Ralph in 'The Society 1876 - 1976' (*Essays in Bristol and Gloucestershire History*, 1976); Bazeley pedigree in Glos. Coll., 6, p.824.

46. Sir Francis Adams HYETT, 1844 - 1941

W.H. Hyett, F.R.S. (1795 - 1877) inherited Painswick House in 1820; his son F.A. Hyett was born in the house and it was his home for ninety-seven years.

Francis Hyett was a man of affairs as well as a scholar. After Eton and Trinity Hall, Cambridge, he practised as a barrister, becoming later Deputy Chairman, 1886 - 1904, and Chairman, 1904 - 1929, of Gloucestershire Quarter Sessions. He was also Vice-Chairman of the County Council from 1904 to 1918, and Chairman from 1918 to 1921. He was knighted in 1919.

With "an eager and enquiring mind, united to an innate passion for accuracy, aided by a phenomenal memory",[1] well-read in classics, history and the arts, Hyett did much for education in Gloucestershire. He had been largely responsible for a printed *Catalogue of County Records*, 1898, which was perhaps the first of its kind to appear in England, and many years later he was the moving spirit in the establishment of the County Records Office in 1936. With all this, he found time for local history and for writing, besides forming one of the most notable private libraries of Gloucestershire. In 1915 he presented 110 volumes of Gloucestershire tracts, pamphlets, etc. — in all, over 3,500 items — to the Gloucester City Library; and most of his local books, including a fine series of rare Civil War tracts, came to the County Records Office after his death. Not only was he a bibliophile, but the *Bibliographer's Manual of Gloucestershire Literature* with its *Supplement*, in which he collaborated successively with Canon Bazeley and Roland Austin, remains as a standard work of permanent value. He was president of the Bristol and Gloucestershire Archaeological Society in 1903, and a frequent contributor to its *Transactions* up to the age of eighty-six.

Publications: *Gloucester and her Governor during the great Civil War*, 1891; *The Civil War in the Forest of Dean*, 1895; *Gloucester in National History*, 1906; *Glimpses of the History of Painswick*, 1928, revised and re-issued 1957; *The Bibliographer's Manual of Gloucestershire Literature* (with Canon William Bazeley), 1895 - 97, and the *Biographical Supplement* (with Roland Austin), 1915 - 16.

MSS. None appear to have been kept, except some minor memoranda now in G.R.O., ref. D. 6.

Biographical sources: *Who was Who* (1941 - 50); obituary in *TBGAS*, lxiii, 267 - 9; W.I. Croome, foreword to Hyett's *Glimpses of the History of Painswick*, revised edition, 1957.

Notes.   1.   W.I. Croome, C.B.E., F.S.A. (see Biographical sources).

47. Charles Samuel TAYLOR, 1848 - 1925

The Reverend C.S. Taylor, F.S.A., joined the Bristol and Gloucestershire Archaeological Society in 1884, edited its *Transactions* from 1894 to 1896 and 1899 to 1914, and was its President for the year 1906. His many well-informed papers in the *Transactions*, extending over twenty-five years, deal mainly with Saxon and Norman Gloucestershire and the ecclesiastical history of Bristol. Taylor's most important work, which has been of value to others up to the present day, is his analysis of the Gloucestershire section of Domesday Book, published by the Society in 1889. In the preface he wrote: "The work has occupied a large part of my leisure time for five years, but it has been a labour thoroughly enjoyed."

Himself a Bristolian — the son of Thomas T. Taylor — he was educated at Rugby and Oxford, returning to be curate at St. Mary Redcliffe, Bristol, 1873 - 77, and Vicar of St. Thomas the Martyr, 1877 - 1896. He then became Vicar of Banwell, Somerset, where he died in the same year as his contemporary pillar of the Archaeological Society, Canon Bazeley.

Publications: *An analysis of the Domesday Survey of Gloucestershire*, 1889; notes on Bristol churches in *Guide to the Church Congress* held at Bristol, 1903; papers in *TBGAS* and *Proc. Clifton Antiquarian Club*.

MSS. None have been traced, except B.R.O., P/St.T/HM 10 and 17: two notebooks, among the records of St. Thomas the Martyr Parish, concerning records of the parish and the church plate and bells.

Biographical sources: obit. in *TBGAS*, xlvi, 383 - 5; Elizabeth Ralph, 'The Society 1876 - 1976', in *Essays in Bristol and Gloucestershire History*, 1976.

48. William Phillimore Watts PHILLIMORE, 1853 - 1913

The family of Phillimore was established at Cam, near Dursley, in the fifteenth century, and they were prosperous clothiers in the eighteenth. A descendant, Dr. W.P. Stiff of Nottingham, who still owned a small farm at Uley, where his ancestors had long dwelt, changed his name and his son's to Phillimore in 1873. The son, W.P.W. Phillimore, became the expert genealogist, well known for his series of printed marriage registers, in which Gloucestershire was the first county to be started. He also edited *Gloucestershire Notes & Queries*, after Beaver Blacker's death, from 1891 to 1901, as well as nos. 85 and 86 in 1904. It was Phillimore who initiated the British Record Society, whose valuable Index Library still continues to grow by degrees. In an article in *Glos. N. & Q.*, in 1893, he advocated the setting up of county record offices, a movement which was to begin thirty years later.

Publications: many, relating to family history, heraldry, etc. Phillimore also edited more than two hundred volumes of parish registers. The following, besides parish registers and articles in *Glos. N. & Q.*, concern Gloucestershire: 'Some notes on Wresden, Uley', in *TBGAS*, xi, 281-90; *Collections relating to the Family of Trotman*, 1892; *Abstracts of Gloucestershire Inquisitions Post Mortem*, 1625 - 1642, ed. W.P.W.P. and G.S. Fry (Index Libr., vols. 9 and 13); *Catalogue of Wills in the Diocese of Gloucester Consistory Court*, ed. W.P.W.P. and L.L. Duncan (Index Libr. Vol. 12); *The "principal genealogical specialist"* (story of Regina v. Davies and the Shipway genealogy, — a pedigree fraud), 1899; *Some account of the Family of Holbrow* (75 copies only), 1901; *Genealogy of the Family of Phillimore*, 1922 (posthumous).

MSS. G.R.O., D.3481. An artificial collection, made by Phillimore, of genealogical material and original documents relating to the Phillimore family and to Gloucestershire.

Biographical sources: 'Some notes on Wresden, Uley' , — see above; *Who's Who*, 1911; *Glos. N. & Q.*, 10, 87 (Apr. 1913), 'In Memoriam'.

49. Frank Step HOCKADAY, 1855 - 1924

After Archdeacon Furney's exploration of the early Gloucester diocesan archives in the eighteenth century, they remained almost undisturbed until after 1900. Their very whereabouts was a matter of some uncertainty, and some seem to have gone astray when the sees of Bristol and Gloucester were temporarily united, between 1836 and 1897.

In 1908 F.S. Hockaday of Lydney, who was collecting material for a history of that town and parish, was puzzled by the lack of early records of the diocese. He at length found them, confused and extremely dirty, in an upper room of the Gloucester Probate Registry, where they had probably lain forgotten since the transfer of probate jurisdiction from Church to State by the Probate Act of 1857.

The history of Lydney was never published, but Hockaday, at the age of 53, had found an occupation for the rest of his life. For sixteen years, to the exclusion of almost every other interest, he toiled at cleaning, sorting, numbering and cataloguing the vast accumulation of books and papers. He mastered the Latin and palaeography required for reading the obscure and abbreviated forms of the Act Books, and pursued the background research which enabled him to understand them. The diocesan authorities were so impressed by his enthusiasm and industry that they eventually allowed him to remove the whole of the records temporarily to a fire-proof store which he had built near his home at Lydney.

The 'Hockaday Abstracts' and indexes, nearly five hundred in number, now in the Gloucester library (whose librarian, Roland Austin, had given Hockaday every possible help and encouragement) have proved of immense value, and are known to everyone who has had occasion to seek information from diocesan sources. They include extensive records relating to the Bristol diocese, to which the indefatigable compiler also turned his attention.

Hockaday's remarkable insight into the history of the Gloucester diocese is evident from his study of the Consistory Court, written just before his death and printed posthumously. He had also transcribed from the Public Record Office and elsewhere numerous manuscripts and abstracted much information concerning the dioceses of both Gloucester and Bristol; and had made valuable contributions on Gloucestershire clergy to the *Alumni Cantabrigienses*, then in course of preparation. His work was recognized by a Fellowship of the Royal Historical Society, and he gave evidence before the Royal Commission on Public Records in 1914.

Publications: 'The Consistory Court of the Diocese of Gloucester', in *TBGAS,* xlvi; 'Withington Peculiar', in *TBGAS,* xl; articles on Lydney parish history, in *Lydney & Aylburton Parish Magazine*, 1907-13.

MSS. Glos Coll.:'Hockaday Abstracts', 456-485 and *passim*, for Gloucester diocese; 5511-12, Bristol diocese; 1272, indexes to the parish registers and transcripts of the diocese of Gloucester (2 vols.); 12144, index of inventories (1586-1856) in Gloucester Probate Registry, etc.

Biographical Sources: Roland Austin, 'Frank Step Hockaday', in *TBGAS*, xlvi, 379-83, and 'The late Mr. F.S. Hockaday and the records of the diocese', in *Gloucester Diocesan Magazine*, Oct. 1924, 116-17; Isabel Kirby, 'Gloucester Diocesan Records', in *TBGAS*, lxxxvii, 119-130.

50. Welbore St. Clair BADDELEY, 1856 - 1946

St. Clair Baddeley (as he was always called), a Justice of the Peace and the son of an army officer, lived for many years at Castle Hale in Painswick, and was a very active amateur historian and archaeologist of literary bent, rather of the nineteenth or even eighteenth century school than of the twentieth. Although he does not appear to have taken a university degree, an honorary LL.D. was conferred upon him in 1933 by the University of St. Andrews, Scotland, as an antiquarian whose "knowledge of architecture and the fine arts laid the foundation for a life's work in archaeology".[1] His artistic and historical interests had been fostered during residence in Italy. In Gloucestershire, besides lecturing, Baddeley took part in excavations at Hailes Abbey (1899) and directed those on the Roman villa site at Ifold in Painswick (1903). A member of the Council of the BGAS for many years, he was President in 1907, but he is said, though genial, to have been somewhat self-opinionated and critical of others, and the disappearance of his name from the membership list some years before his death may have been due to disagreements. Some of his considerable printed work, in particular his history of Cirencester, gives a great deal of information, not always marshalled very clearly.

Publications: *History of the Church of St. Mary, at Painswick*, 1902; *A Cotteswold Manor* [Painswick], 1907; *A Cotteswold Shrine* [Hailes Abbey], 1908; *Place-Names of Gloucestershire: A Handbook*, 1913; *A History of Cirencester*, 1924; many papers in *TBGAS*; poems, literary works concerning Italy, etc. The *Catalogue of the Gloucestershire Collection* lists 58 of Baddeley's publications.

MSS. Glos. Coll., Baddeley Collection: notebooks, including personal diaries, anecdotes, travel journals, and antiquarian notes, nearly all ill-written, untidy and confused, but containing much of interest. The Gloucester Library also has (Glos. Coll. Suppt., vol. 1, 107) the author's copy of *Place-Names of Gloucestershire*, with MS. annotations.

Biographical Sources: *Who's Who in Gloucestershire*, 1934; Burke's

Landed Gentry, 1937; Kelly's Handbook, 1938; obituary (brief) in *Gloucester Citizen*, 1946.

Notes. 1. It appears that Sir James Irvine, then Principal of St. Andrews, while on a motoring tour of the Cotswolds with Sir David Russell, F.S.A., was admiring Castle Hale, when Baddeley invited them in. They were so impressed by this "courteous and learned old man" that Irvine felt his work merited academic recognition, and obtained his nomination for an honorary doctorate. (Information kindly given by the Keeper of the Muniments, St. Andrews University, from recollections of a contemporary).

51. William Henry KNOWLES, 1857 - 1943

Northumberland may have a better claim than Gloucestershire to W.H. Knowles, for he practised as an architect in Newcastle-upon-Tyne, his birthplace, for nearly forty years. His hobby was archaeology, and besides contributing to the History of Northumberland he directed important excavations on Hadrian's Wall.

Retiring to Cheltenham in 1922, at the age of 65 but still in full vigour, Knowles soon became an active and valued member of the Bristol and Gloucestershire Archaeological Society, helping in the arrangements for excursions, doing pioneer work in the listing of historic buildings, supervising and writing reports on 'digs' in Gloucester, at Deerhurst, and on Leckhampton Hill, and inspiring younger members to the systematic excavation of prehistoric and Romano-British sites. It was he who founded the Roman Research Committee for Gloucester, which did good work long after his time. He acted both as Chairman of Council of the B. & G.A.S. and (in 1930-31) as President. The many papers written for the Society's *Transactions* by this learned student of architectural history are to be found in Volumes xlvii to lx; those on Deerhurst Church, The Gloucester Blackfriars, 'The Development of Architecture in Gloucestershire to the Close of the 12th Century', and The Roman Baths at Bath are among the most important. The writer of Knowles's obituary notice in the *Transactions* said that it was difficult to refer to all that he had done for the Society.

In addition, he was a link between Gloucestershire and national institutions. A Fellow of the Society of Antiquaries from 1899, he served on its Council in 1921 and again in 1926, on the Architectural Committee of the Victoria County History, and on the Central Council for the Care of Churches.

Publications: Knowles wrote no books, but a great many papers. His two reports, in collaboration with R.H. Forster, on the excavations at Corstopitum (Corbridge-on-Tyne) were issued in 1909.

MSS. The existence of manuscript material has not been traced.

Biographical sources: *TBGAS*, lxiii, 271-4; *Archaeologia Aeliana*, 4th ser., vol. 21 (1943), 248-53; Elizabeth Ralph, 'The Society 1876-1976', in *Essays in Bristol and Gloucestershire History*, 1976, pp. 25-37, 45.

52. Roland AUSTIN, 1874 - 1954

A native of Reading, Roland Austin became City Librarian of Gloucester in his twenties, and during his time there (1900 - 1936) built up an outstanding collection of Gloucestershire books and manuscripts, his monumental catalogue of which was published with the aid of the Carnegie Trustees in 1928. The Bristol and Gloucestershire Archaeological Society owed much to him as its Honorary Secretary 1917 - 28, Treasurer 1924 - 28 and 1937 - 44, Librarian 1923 - 48, and President during the war years 1939 - 1944. He had also been Secretary of the Cotteswold Naturalists' Field Club from 1916 to 1919. One of the founders of the quarterly review *Antiquity*, to which he gave its name, he was its joint editor with the archaeologist O.G.S. Crawford from 1927 to 1948.

Persuaded by his friend Sir Francis Hyett (with whom he had collaborated in bibliographical work) to organise a County Records Office for Gloucestershire, he left the City Library in 1936 at the age of 62.[1] Although the second world war came all too soon, he was able in war-time to rescue quantities of historical records from what was ironically known as 'salvage', and thus to lay the foundation of future developments before finally retiring in 1948. Austin was made an honorary M.A. of Bristol University in 1927 and elected F.S.A. in 1928. In his last years, depressed by the accidental death of his daughter, who was County Librarian, he became morose and difficult, but the sterling work of his prime should not be forgotten. It included valuable papers on local history in the *Transactions* of the Bristol & Gloucestershire Society, the Cotteswold Field Club's *Proceedings*, and elsewhere.

Publications: *Some Gloucestershire Books and their writers*, 1911; *Samuel Rudder* (reprinted from *The Library*, 1915); *Biographical Supplement to the Bibliographer's Manual of Gloucestershire Literature* (with F.A. Hyett), 1915-16; *Painswick House Collection* (catalogue of books presented by F.A. Hyett to the Gloucester Public Library), 1916; *History of the Gloucester Journal, 1722-1922*, 1922; *Catalogue of the Gloucestershire Collection*, 1928; *The Crypt School, Gloucester, 1539-1939*, 1939; numerous papers in *TBGAS*, *Proc. C.N.F.C.*, *N. & Q.*, *The Library*, etc.

MSS. Austin does not appear to have left any of his working papers to the Archaeological Society or the City Library; he may have destroyed them. The Lindsay Fleming Collection now in Yale University Library ('Lysons boxes') has some 60 letters from Roland Austin to Lindsay Fleming, on the Lysons family.

Biographical sources: *Who Was Who*, 1960; obituary (rather inadequate) in *TBGAS*, lxxiii, 242-3; Elizabeth Ralph, 'The Society 1876-1976', in *Essays in Bristol and Gloucestershire History*, 1976.

Note. 1. His change of allegiance, without warning, caused a breach of relations between Austin and the City, and for about twelve years he did not set foot in the library where he had worked so long and with such distinction.

ILLUSTRATIONS OF HANDWRITING

1a. WILLIAM WORCESTRE
A note on Cirencester etc, 1480
(Worcestre's Itineraries, Corpus Christi, Cambridge, MS.210, f.205)

1a. *William Worcestre*

(The transcript is taken by permission from Dr. J.H. Harvey's edition of Worcestre's Itineraries, 1969)

Cyrencestre

Longitudo ecclesie parochialis Sancti ---- in villa de Cyssetyr alias Cirencestre cum choro continet 90 gressus

latitudo dicte ecclesie continet cum duobus alis 50 gressus

longitudo campanilis dicte ecclesie continet 7 virgas

latitudo turris sine spera continet 6 virgas et dimidium

Caput fontis primi fluminis Tamisie ex parte ville Cissetyr incipit per 3 miliaria de villa Tetberye in comitatu Glouc^r apud villam de Kenylle apud capellam vocatam Tewelle in dicta parochia et nunquam dictus fons desiccatur in maxima siccitate anni

Cotys villa

Cotiswold mons sortitur nomen et distat per 3 miliaria de Cyssetyr prope le Fosseway versus Bristolliam

Cirencester

The length of the parish church of St. ---- in the town of Ciceter, otherwise Cirencester, is 90 paces including the choir

The width of the said church, with the two aisles, is 50 paces

The length of the belfry of the said church is 7 yards

The width of the tower, which has no spire, is 6½ yards

The source of the first spring of the River Thames in the neighbourhood of Cirencester rises 3 miles from the town of Tetbury in Gloucestershire at the township of Kemble, at a chapel called Tewelle[1] in the said parish, and the said spring never goes dry in the greatest drought of the year

Coates township
 [from which] the Cotswold Hills take their name, is distant 3 miles from Cirencester towards Bristol, near the Foss Way

1. Now Ewen, derived from Aet Ewelme, 'at the source' (E.P.N.S., Place-Names of Gloucestershire, I, 276).

1b. WILLIAM WORCESTRE
Letter to Churchwardens of Oxenton, Glos, [1456]
(G.R.O., D1637 M13)

1b. William Worcestre

Welbelovyd frendys I grete yow well and lete yow wete that I have spoke wyth my lord bysshop of Worcestr Chauncellor that the processe and cause that the Aumoner of Tewkysbury hath ayenst yow myght be contynewed tille Mydsomer or Myghellmasse next commyng; so that yn the mene tyme the materes that ye be troubled for may be examyned and determyned here at London by indyfferent lerned men chosen by agreement of the Aumoner and of my lord ys councell. And my seyd lord ys chauncellor seyth he wolle comyn [commune] wyth the Aumoner and meove hym to do soo. And by thys wey it shall be leest cost and trouble cesed: but ye most doo sende a remembraunce yn wrytyng to London of all all (sic) your ryght and the customs of the contree deuly approuved. My lord[1] myght trouble the abbot of Tewkysbury more than the Aumoner wenyth yff he woold. More over I have remembred my lord to geve a chesyple[2] to your chyrch because ye be febly purveyed, and trust for certeyn ye shall have one. And ye shuld hafe had a coope [cope] also safe for the trouble that your parson makyth ayenst yow. And y have a cloth of sylk redye delyvered me for yow. And shall put it to makyng. And ye, Thomas Wattes, that ye sende to Castelcombe xii goode lampreys poudred[3] at the p(ry)ce of xx d. the pece. And they of Castelcombe shall send hem to London. And foryete not a couple godc lampreys for my labour yn recoveryng the vii li [£7] that ye had allmoste lost of my lordys money - for ye know well the baylly had spent it awey — and let my lampreys com wyth the othyr lampreys. And yff the (?propters)[4] of your chyrch sende me mo lampreys for me and my felowys y shall the better thynk uppon your vestment. Recommaund me to maister Moreyn and let hym see thys lettre. God kepe yow. Wryt at London the xvi day of March

by William Worcestre[5]

1. Worcestre's employer, Sir John Fastolf, was lord of the manor of Oxenton, Glos.; the ecclesiastical living belonged to Tewkesbury Abbey. It seems that Fastolf had backed the parishioners against the monks in a dispute about tithe.
2. chasuble   3. salted or cured   4. ?appropriators (the Abbot and monks of Tewkesbury)
5. This interesting and amusing letter, found attached to a manorial record of Oxenton, was published by the late Dr. K.B. McFarlane in *Medium Aevum,* Vol. xxxi (1962), but a photograph of the original has not before been reproduced.

Henricus Vaghan Mayor
Johnes Stephens Vic
Johnes Vaghan ⎫ Balli
Willimus Fannicott ⎭

This yere the vijth day of Octobre was the grettest flode & the grettist wynde at Bristowe & in the contrey there abowte that evir was seyn. And grete hurt doon in mthymty fellers in wode & salt. Shippes lost at kyngrade the Anthony of Bristowe & a ship of Bilbowe set alond at Holow bak{e} & other botes oo{er} the cost. Saltmyssh down come catell & houses borne away w{ith} the see. And moche people drowned to the nomebre of xl or mo. And sone after Henry Duc of Buk{e} was biheded at Saz

Willimus Bykelyn Mayor
Johes Wayno Vic
Johnes Hemmyng ⎫ Balli
Willimus Spycer ⎭

This yere Havvy Erle of Richmonnt londed at Milford Haven in Wales. And sone after mette with king Richard at Bosworth feld. And there gate the feld of king Richard the xxijth day of August where the same king Richard was slayne. And sone after there was a sodeyn siknes in all places of England called the swetyng sythes. Wherof moche people dyed.

2. Robert Ricart

(1484) Henricus Vaghan maior
Joh(an)nes Stephens vic' [sheriff]
Joh(an)nes Vaghan   }
Will(el)mus Gauncell } Ball(iv)i [bailiffs]

This yere the xvth day of Octobre was the grettest flode & the grettist wynde at Bristowe & in the cuntrey there aboutes that ever was seen. And grete hurt doon in marchauntes sellers in woode & salt, shippes lost at Kyngrode
the Anthony of Bristowe & a ship of Bilbowe [Bilbao] set alond[1]
at Holow bakkes, & other botes & cokkes lost. Saltmarssh drowned,
corne catell & houses borne awey w^t [with] the see. And moche
people drowned to the nommebre of CC & mo. And sone after Henry Duc of Buk[ingham] was bihedded at Sarum

(1485) Wil(el)mus Wikeham Maior
Joh(ann)es Swayne vic'
Joh(an)nes Hemmyng   }
Will(el)mus Spycer   } ball(iv)i

This yere Harry Erle of Richmount londed at Milford haven in Wales. And sone after he mette with King Richard
at Bosworth feld and there gate the feld of King Richard the xxiith day of August where the same King Richard was slayne. And sone after there was a sodeyn sikenes in all places of Englond called the sweting syknes, wherof moche people dyed.

> A marginal note against the entry for 1484 adds:
> 'And this yer the two sonnes of King E[dward] were put to seylence in the towre of London'

[1]driven ashore

Rules for ye keepinge my Clocke

If ye clocke goe too slow: ye spring upon ye plomet on ye
leaft hand. And if it goe fast, abate [one] of ye changs from of ye
hand I cannot. Even by what thing from ye ordr̃ waight or a Spring of ye

If ye hole of ye clocke goe before ye moon or under ye diall, will
by ye waight on ye right hand, And if ye under [   ] it
come to ye [   ] ye Iron [   ] [   ] goe by it [   ] And ye voice ye
needle [   ] ye [   ] on plate of ye clocke

If ye needle of ye Squeere before ye [hole] of ye clocke run to ye clocke
to[o] farre, nor it come to ye [   ] [hole]

If bee ye hole of ye clocke [   ] C ye needle to ye [   ], set off ye hand and from lot ye one
forwards together, [   ] ye needle will goe right, As try about at ffyre [   ] ye clocke
to make come if ye waight are more of some fashion of

3. JOHN SMITH (of Nibley)
'Rules for the kepinge my clocke'

3. *John Smith of Nibley*

Rules for the kepinge my clocke

If the clocke goe too slowe hange more waight upon the plomet on the
least hand: And if it goe too fast, abate some of the waight from of[f] the
same plomet eyther by abatinge from the greater waight or by addynge to the lesse.

If the stroke of the clocke goe before the gnomon or nedle of the diall take
of[f] the waight on the right hand, And let the nedle runne till it come to the houre where you would have it stay. And soe will the needle overtake the hammer or st[r]oke of the clocke

If the needle of the dyall be before the stroke of the clocke, cause the clocke
to stryke till it come to the nedle

If bothe the stroke of the cloke & the needle be togeather, yet both too backward, then let both runne
forward togeather. And the needle will goe right as fast about as thou causest the clocke to strike: because the waightes are none of them taken of[f].

He adds further on: "To spunge the clocke from dust, doe it with feathers and by blowinge with a bellowes" ready, yet they durst not come forth, but stayed to put on the other of them first. Our men (seeing there no[t] provision of their Captains) marched away to the place and showe appointed, attended by the Maior & Aldermen and many Knights and gentlemen, whome they placed in a faire tent, as spectatours and iudges for the business. There our men shewed 2 bowes for the comming of Exeter men, who at last with much intreatie of those gentlemen came. The winde blew hard at southwest all that day, which so much disturbed their sandes on each side, that of 52 shotts on both sides, that our men shott but 7 bulletts into the target, and they put in 5 shotts. Then night overtaking them before of each side were loft to shoot for triall the next day one shott, a peece, so for that time they rested.

The next morning they all met there againe, and the wind was then calmer, & we of our men shott into the target, and they forth shott but one with eight ouer it, and never a one of theirs of men come within halfe a foot of them. So our men were best ioyned, and theirs, wonne all the three wounds, and 1008 in money, but the betts wonne on our side came unto a great deale more. Our Captaines willed theire Treasurer of Exeter to put every penny to accompts with they said laid out in our Cittie that time, and required them againe, spending that 1008 that they wonne and so much more vppon them, to double requit theire curtesie, not suffering them to give ought to any officer or powre in our Cittie. So on friday after dinner they all tooke horse, and our men accompanied them good part of the way.

George Harrington Maior { Mathew Warren } Shiriffes.
                        { William Turner   }

The Carke of Bristoll was newly pitched from one end to the other, & the walles & steppes repaired and mended.

In the yeare before Sir Walter Rawley made his last voyadge to the west Indies, and this yeare in the Whitson[tide] for returned, and put into Kinsale in Ireland, & afterward went to London & was there imprisoned in the Towre.

4. WILLIAM ADAMS
The Bristol v. Exeter shooting-match, etc., 1616—18
(Adams's Chronicle, B.R.O. 13748(4))

4. William Adams

(1616)
ready, yet they durst not come forth, but strived to put one the other of them foremost. Our men (seeing that no perswasion of theire Captaines could move them) marched away to the place and howre appointed, attended by the Maior & Councell and many knights and gentlemen, whome they placed in a faire tent, as expectatours and iudges for the buisines. There our men taried 2 howres for the coming of Exeter men, who at last with much intreatie of theire gentlemen came. The wind blew hard at sowthwest all that day, wch so much disturbed theire hands on each side, that of 52 shotts, on both sides, that our men shott 7 bulletts into the target, and they put in 5 shotts. Then night overtaking them fowre of each side were left to showt for triall the next day one shott a peece, so for that time they rested.

The next morning they all met there againe, and the winde was then calme. Three of our men shott into the target, and the fowrth shott but one inch right over it, and never a one of theire 4 men came within halfe a foot of them. So our men were best, second, and third, wonne all the three rowndes and 100s. in money, but the betts wonne on our side came unto a great deale more. Our Captaines willed theire Treasurer of Exeter to put every penny to accompt wch they had laid out in our Cittie that time, and repaid them againe, spending that 100s. that they wonne and so much more upon them, to double requit theire curtesie, not suffering them to give ought to any officer or poore in our Cittie. So on friday after dinner they all tooke horse, and our men accompanied them good part of the way.

(1617)
George Harrington Maior { Mathew Warren / William Turner } Shirifes

The backe of Bristoll was newly pitched from one end to the other, & the walles & slippes repaired and mended.

In the yeare before Sr Walter Rawley made his last voyadge to the west Indies, and this yeare in the Whitson weke he returned, and put into Kinsale in Ireland, & afterwards went to London & was there imprisoned in the towre.

Dear Sir,

I shall be glad of an opportunity to express to you personally my sincerest thanks for your kind communication of yesterday. I am very much obliged by the kindness of one of my friends in Washington (George J. Abbot Esqr.) for enabling me to make a comparison of my sketch of General [Wm.] Lee Davidson (whose life I am about to write), I shall be much obliged if you will have the kindness to forward them

faithfully yours
John Thier[?]

Captn. Fr[a]s M. Ford
July 1852

—

that I have secured his likeness of my kinsman, it is not easy to express my high sense of the favor. If you can add anything to my store of anecdotes respecting the General & his family, it would be especially acceptable. Among his Descendants are many who hold respectable positions in society.

G. A. Davidson

You may direct to care of Capt. E. M. Ford from wear at George[town] in Washington.

5. John Theyer

Mr Wood

That yow have procured my booke out of the Lo:[rd] Farefax hands, yow have done me an especiall favour, it havinge ben my care a longe tyme to obtayne it. Yo^r l[ett]re also was pleasinge to me, in regard I thereby collect yow are all well, especially yor mother my old freind. To make a Catalogue of my MS (beinge many) will require a longe tyme, therefore I desier that yow ?ratify me in 2 or 3 lines the particulers of the subject yow are upon (for I have almost forgotten yor designe therein) & I shall reddily communicate unto yow whatsoever I have (if any such be in my studdy) conduceinge to yor purpose. And of this yow may be fully assured from

    Yo^r affeccionate freind & Servt
    John Theyer

Cowpers hill neare Glouc^r
2 Febr 1662

    Yow may direct yor l[ett]re to be left for me at the George in Ciceter

Sir

I can give you ffirst as he sett down ffirmerly the Grandfa[ther]
in... names, and what Towne he, his wife was
an Istrum, and how many children they had, and
wives they have married, and which ffsons, and
holy
....esses names, and hair ffsus, G, which
...a married to Totnfs, yor ffend and Servant

Ab. Wantner

Northcerney. Glouc. Vale. Westwood

T. Smith at 10—5. 0s.
Rects. 2—3—0.
Proxie. 0—6—8.   to Woodmancote, two hamletts, whereof Synods. 0—2—0.   huius.   one were Chappells
P.Rolls. at f. west 4d.   6 Calender   but now demolished.

There are 14 Acres and an halfe of Arable and lying in ye
Common feilds. belonging to ye Poor. But tis but Cursus terrae
yt tis lett for it & or 18 s. an Acre at most.

In Northcerney feilds there is a Campe.
Coteys Berr is a fayr heap of stones yt groweth on ye top of
an hill betweene at a great distance.

In Calmisden feilds was plowed up a Roman Vrn & of Bones
wth glasse full of Ashes
there was ye Chappell of our Blessed Lady of Kery.

7. RICHARD PARSONS
(Part) description of North Cerney, from his 'Parochial Visitation'
(Bodl. MS. Rawl., B323, f.56)

and fully to be compleated and ended **yeelding** and paying therefore unto the said Iu[...] of Ou'pp'er Swell if it be then Iu[...] the [...]tent ion of the p'misses and may be thirby enabled to accept and [...]inessbly have h'eunto sett their hands and Seales the day and

Robert   At Kyn, jun'

8. SIR ROBERT ATKYNS, jun.
Signature on deed, 1702
(G.R.O., D2113/2)

Cheltenham, ads Chiltenham, and Chiltham, is a Towne scituate on ye North side of a small purling silver-streame or Rivulet called Chilt, from wh: Rivulet ye Saxons gave it ye name of Chiltham, ye word ham wth them being the same as ye word Towne is amongst us. It is the frontier of the Cottswolde side of one of the most fertile vallies my world, and an ancient markett Towne a good league from ye Gloucestrian Nilus or reverse of Cotswold hill, standing abt it North East, East, & South East in a semicircle or like a halfe moone. It's soile is sandy and very naturall for carrets, cabbage, & Turnips, insomuch that the whole neighbourhood for sundry miles round it is annually furnished with these three from this Towne, ye but street continued wth buildings one on each side for a full mile in length. it has but one church but that large & built of goodly stone, bothe

9. JOHN PRINN or PRYNNE
From memoranda in Cheltenham Manor Court Book
(G.R.O., D655 M12)

Sr,

Being lately in my Study I had not time to look over ye Copys, before they went to be bound; only I run over the Sonday, in which you had take a great deal of pains, and we together will be y[our]e Sr, extremely usefull in any thing ye Book I shall as soon as some of the Profess, or some very well posed to find any left likely to stay 2 or 3 days among your Friends; but could wish you had omitted some Epitaph's, w[hi]ch I am very sorry to say self, & not belong to me; however, as you are a hand then at of friendly and ?oping of those ?em of ?ank, and a very fit ?olum, upon them.

Pag: 20 or 3, Lex. has a Lexicon in the Body of ye Booke, it has a Book in pag. 8, op. 20 or Lex. has very pretty intimate of ye Copy; I should be very heartily glad if you ?a so ?a advance[d] ?a one[?]; if you ?a go into a ?a or a ?a of[?] some ?a one[?] will serve ye way, by the first opportunity. Rich will ?a ?a ?a ?a Ready for a ?a January, 4 from Sr, Yo[u]rs &c ?a Respects,
        Richard Graves.

Mickleton, 29 of June, 1723.

10. Richard Graves

Being so taken up I had not time to look over the copies, before they went to be bound; onely I run over the Contents, in which you have taken a great deal of Pains; and are together with the Index, extremely useful in understanding the Book; And also run over some of the Preface, and am very well pleased to find myself likely to stand recorded among your Friends; but could wish you had omitted some Epithets, which I am conscious to my self, do not belong to me; however, as you meant them out of Kindness and Respect, I take 'em as such; and accordingly return you Thanks.

There are 2 or 3 Gentlemen have seen the Books lye in the Bookbinder's Shop, and have been very pressing with me to gett them copies; I doubt, S^r you have none left; otherwise, I should be extremely thankfull, if you could help me to 2 or 3, or more copies; and I will return the money by the first opportunity; this, with my most kind Respects, and Thanks for all Favours, is all from
    Dear S^r
    Your most obliged humble serv^t
      Richard Graves
Mickleton, 29th June, 1723

In the first part of the letter, Graves apologizes for delay in acknowledging books, being "under a sort of fatigue of late of visiting and being visitted", followed by a fever and sore throat.

There is a post-script: At present I can't recollect anything about R[obert] of Glr., but I reckon I have mett with something about him; I shall, be sure, be mindfull of it . . .

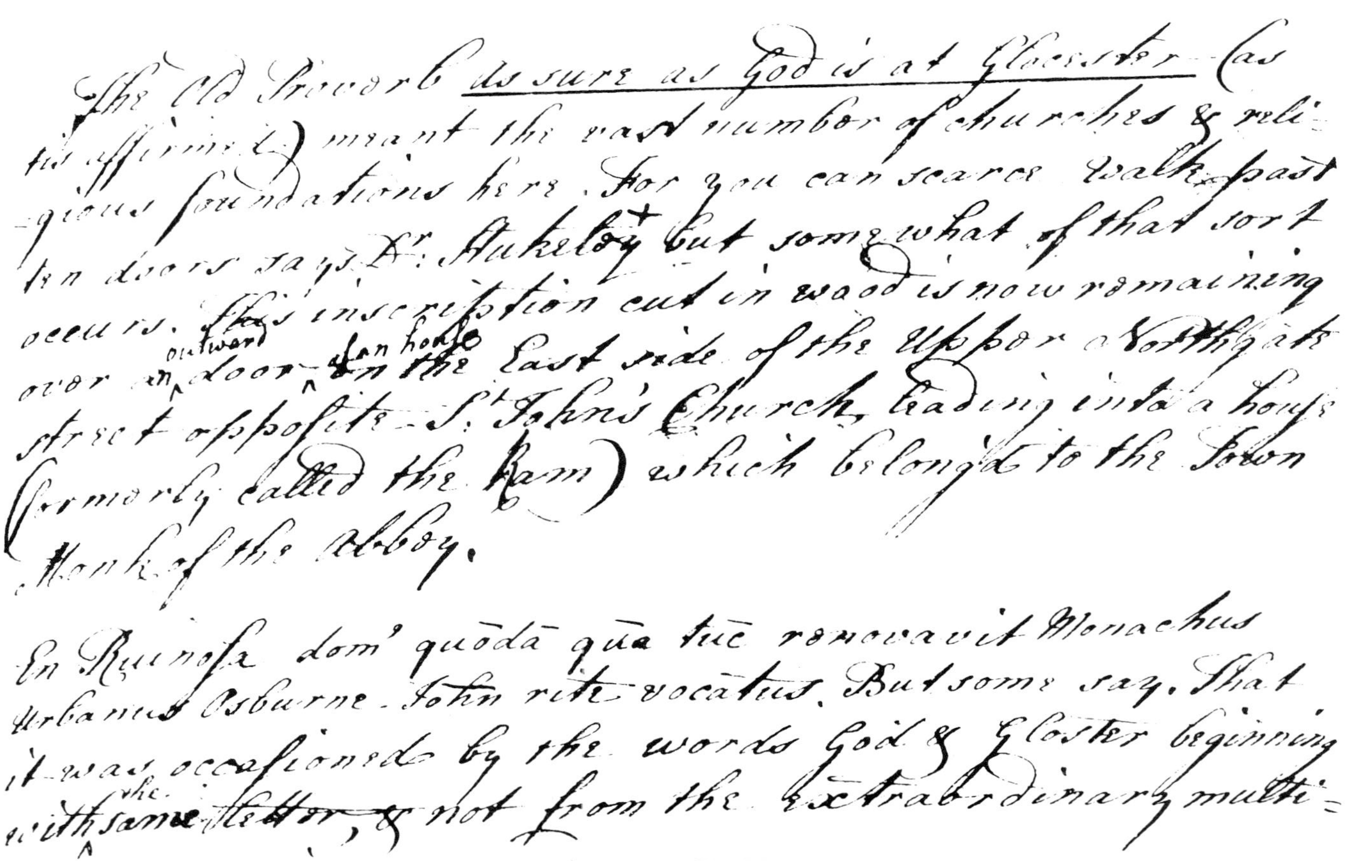

The Old Proverb As sure as God is at Glocester (as 'tis affirm'd) meant the vast number of churches & reli=
gious foundations here. For you can scarce walk past
ten doors says Dr. Stukeley† but somewhat of that sort
occurs. This inscription cut in wood is now remaining
over an outward door of an house on the East side of the Upper or Northgate
street opposite St. John's Church, leading into a house
(formerly called the Ram) which belong'd to the Saxon
Monks of the Abbey.

En Ruinosa dom' quodā quā tūc renovavit Monachus
Urbanus Osburne John rite vocatus. But some say. That
it was occasioned by the words God & Gloster beginning
with the same letter, & not from the extraordinary multi=

11. RICHARD FURNEY

Sr.: your Letter of July the 1st wherein you were pleas'd to inform me (what I always thought) that Mr. Graves designed his Collections should be preserv'd in his Family: however since they are parted with, I am highly pleas'd they are come into such Honourable hands. If you have not seen Mr. Graves's Epitaph, or are desirous of seeing it, be pleas'd to let me know, and I will send you the Inscriptions, and a drawing of the Monument. Mr. West inform'd me that he compos'd the Inscription. The Coins that I met with at Cirencester are of Julia Constantia (Emp. to Constantius Gallus) of Arcadius and Honorius, with some gold Coins of the Constantine Family, with Reverses that I had not met with before.

which with my most humble Service
is all in great hast from,
    Sir,
        Your most oblig'd humble Servant,
            Geo: Ballard.

Campden
July the 18.
1732.

12. GEORGE BALLARD
Letter (abbreviated) to Thomas Hearne, 1732
(Bodl., Rawl. lett. 6(S.C.15572) 2/249

Owing to my being lately engaged in the Neighbourhood of Bristol, I have not been long returned to this Place, otherwise I should have answered your esteemed Favour before this Time. Inasmuch obliged to Mr Stocky favourable Recommendation of me. I have never advertized publishing my Intentions frequently; Sr Robt Atkins's History, with Additions, but owing to the sadness I have had in this office, have not yet been with this Last as one intended, and Mr Rudder having forestalled me. While now to model my Publication and make it rather more an History of the Inhabitants than of the Shire to let as from each of the Shire shall give. To each Parish will be given an authentic Information can be obtained, the intended the Pedigrees of such Families which have been anciently worshipful or Recd of Property are now settled therein. Therefore Sir I shall esteem it an honour to be favoured with your Family Pedigree & Connections to add to the great Number I have received.

13. RALPH BIGLAND
From a letter to the Rev. H.G. Dobyns-Yate, 1780
(G.R.O., Pc.179)

XX The Asteria Columnaris, a pentangular stone, about the thickness of a large goose-quill, with a stop of five radii at each end, is found at Aston-Ingham in this parish; and I have seen the grinders of an elephant in the tooerand MC Catcott's collection of fossils at Bristol, which I am informed was taken out of the pit at that place.

To what has been said of the natural oil of the parish, and the produce of the ground upon the surface, I must add, that below it there are inexhaustible treasures of iron-ore and cinders, pit-coal, red and yellow ochre, lime-stone, &c. And there is a large furnace for smelting the iron-ore, and several forges for manufacturing of iron, all belonging to Mr. Bathurst.

There is a place called the Scowells, in a wood about a mile above the gentleman's house. It is a cavern, the entrance to which is between very long unwrought stones, which serve as pillars to support a rocky roof, with several bays trees growing upon it. The space within the cavern is about sixteen or eighteen feet broad and beautifully lined with various kinds of moss, which is supposed to have a down spontaneously to the present thickness of two or three inches. Tradition is entirely silent as to this place, and no traveller has taken notice of it.

14. SAMUEL RUDDER
From a draft description of Lydney, n.d., sent to Charles Bragge Bathurst, n.d.
(G.R.O., D421 E27)

The Country smiles around me — "Corn fields richly crept The verdant Buddings of Trees Blossoming of Violets smelling of Birds singing, the Cocks crowing, the Geese cackling, of Turkies gobbling, the Hens clucking, & chickens chirping all these salute my ears, homely a feast mine eyes alone. all Nature looks Gay, & every thing conspires to gladden the Heart & raise & Imagination that even if with a Genius planted by age & broken by Disease am almost inspir'd with Poetic fire to describe the Rural felicity here to be enjoy'd. by a mind rightly dispos'd. in a Body free from pain. — But I would escape from these towering Thoughts & confine them to the strict path of History without deviating into fields of harangue, — of which I shall for that purpose

15. WILLIAM BARRETT
From a letter to George Catcott, 1788

-- 31. Elizabeth Wife of Thomas Harris buried
Jan.y 7. Henry Son of John & Elizabeth Kirtch baptized
-- 21. Anne Daughter of Abraham & **Anne** P[...]
-- 28. Henry Son of John & Elizabeth Kirth buried
Dec.r 19. Jane Daughter of John & Anne Hier baptized
-- 17. James Son of John & Mary Crane baptized
-- 29. Mary Yeats buried --
            Tho.s Rudge, B.D., Rector.

16. THOMAS RUDGE

From the parish register of St. Michael's, Gloucester, 1784
(G.R.O., P154/14 1N1/3)

The Rector is evidently proud of his B.D. degree, which he had received that year.

A letter which I rec'd yesterday from Mr Blore, ~~occasion~~ inclosing one wh he rec'd from yr Lordship, has given me excessive uneasiness. That I sh'd make a second mistake, on the same subject, & this last so palpable, is a more unpleasant circumstance, than any wh has happened during the whole publication. It is besides so extraordinary, that I shall scarcely beli that the error is mine until I see my o handwriting against me. And if I ha made such a mistake, I sh'd have supp that Mr Blore w'd have observed it; p ticularly since he is a Clergyman's son & his wife a Clergyman's daughter; & in

17. SAMUEL SEYER
From a draft letter to the Bishop of Bristol, Feb. 1822
(B.R.O., 12147/52)

An author's misfortune. Seyer's illustrator, Edward Blore F.R.S., had sent a proof-print of a plate to the Bishop, who replied pointing out that the [somewhat fulsome] dedication omitted to mention that he was Bishop of Bristol. Seyer (the Bishop's chaplain!) is in a terrible fluster.

18. GEORGE WORRALL COUNSEL
Letter to Sir Thomas Phillipps about a sale of Furney manuscripts, 1834
(Bodl. MS. Phillipps-Robinson, c.451, fol.108)
For the reply see Ill. no. 32.

19. DANIEL LYSONS
(Part of) draft letter to Charles Bragge Bathurst, n.d. concerning

20. SAMUEL LYSONS
Drawing of font from St. Mary de Crypt, Gloucester, n.d.
(Soc. of Antiquaries, MS. 782/7)

My dear Sir

Allow me to express my thanks for your late attentions to me, and the gratification I received from the inspection of your singularly beautiful Gothic library.

Since we conversed respecting the decoration of the ceiling, I have made a selection of forty five coats of the principal Boistoreans, during six centuries, which may be disposed in the pannels, according to their dates. as I have allotted nine each to a century. If two

21. JAMES DALLAWAY
(Part of) letter to G.W. Braikenridge, from Leatherhead, 15 July 1828
(Bris. L., 23999)
For the Gothic Library, see the section on Braikenridge (no. 24)

Blasoned in their proportions by my dear neice Sophia Phelps. Febr. 26 1841

J.D. Phelps

22. JOHN DELAFIELD PHELPS

Note on fly-leaf of *A Collection of Coats of Arms . . . of Gloucestershire*, 1792, with shields hand-coloured.

(Gloucester library, Clifford Collection)

The artistic accomplishments of Victorian young ladies were often employed by antiquarian fathers or uncles; cf. George Ormerod (no. 27)

Sir/

I sent you the enclosed in order that you may do me (if you think pro-
-per) the honor and kindness of filling up the blanks. You will have
the satisfaction of seeing that the pedigree of Clifford of Frampton
down to the Clintextuches of Eastington, no longer labours under
that deficiency, of which M. Nicolas complains. The pedigree of Cl-
-interbrook is also in the British Museum, but the laws of that
institution forbid the copy of any one M.S. completely, and
I was obliged to omit some pedigrees, where the property was not
material.* Should you think proper to have the pedigree engraved
for the work, which you might have done by my Engraver
for a very trifling expence, I will supply the arms, & often ma-
-tters, or about the work with your patronage among your friends,
you will confer an additional favour, on him, who is

Sir/
Your Obliged humble servant
Tho. Dudley Fosbrooke.

Horsley June 4. 1802 —

* I copied 156. unprinted pedigrees: I have in the whole about 160.

23. THOMAS DUDLEY FOSBROKE (né FOSBROOKE)
Letter to Nathaniel Clifford of Frampton, 1802, about the *History of Gloucestershire*

My dear Sir,

I have to acknowledge the receipt of your Favors of 15th. and 31st. Decemr. your parcels for Tyson, and the Bristol Institution, I delivered on their own; and I have circulated every Prospectus you have sent me to the present time. I am aware of the pecuniary obligations which will be required of him on being elected a Fellow, and I am perfectly convinced we have not in this City a more zealous Antiquary than he is. He would feel highly gratified I am sure at being named and if you will

24. GEORGE WEARE BRAIKENRIDGE
(Part of) letter to John Britton, F.S.A., 15 Jan. 1830, about the proposal of
William Tyson for the Fellowship of the Society of Antiquaries.
(Bris. L. 22992)

25. PAUL HAWKINS FISHER

Notes on Stroud church, n.d. (G.R.O., D1842, H2)

"The oak table now in the Vestry used to stand, as a Communion Table, against the stone work under the East Window of the South Aisle where Mr. Stephens' monument once stood. Old John Pitt said he as a boy say (8 years old) helped his father (John Pitt the eldest) when he removed Stephens' monument from its former place. This was (probably) when the Gallery there was put up and the window made. Old John Pitt was 70 odd years old when he died".

The Bristol Memorialist was originally projected by Mr Tyson. The literary friend to whom he proposed to join him in the undertaking as mentioned in the advertisement was the rev'd — the learned author of the Consever and some minor works relating to the history and topography of Bristol.

Three numbers were published under their joint editorship, the fourth

26. JOHN EVANS
From note inserted in copy of Tyson's *Bristol Memorialist*
(Glos. Coll. 5353)

St Keynsmarks, continued Unitedley & subsequent purchase to Piercefield Estate

The property of Colwood of Piercefield in 1804. (ope)

Sold among other outlying parts of Piercefield by Mr Wells in 18__

to ~~C____ K____~~

Purchased by Thomas Key, ~~Clepstow~~ Chepstow the owner in 1864

Geo O

27. GEORGE ORMEROD
Note on records of Beachley and Chepstow area
(from volume in possession of Mr P.J. Ormerod, 1979)

Gent:—

I have taken the earliest opportunity of forwarding you my sixth number of the Tewkesbury Register and Magazine — which I beg your acceptance of.

I am, much obliged,
Yours,
Bennett

Tewkesbury, 30 June 1834.

28. JAMES BENNETT
Note, presenting book to Nichols & Son, publishers.
(In British Library copy of Bennett's *Tewkesbury Register*)

In 1552 the Taverns in Bristol were reduced to
Six, by Act of Parliam.t — By what were their
Names and situations?

Does the Full Moon in Stokes Croft belong to the
corporation? If so, any particulars about it —
but died the day after he was sworn
In 1683 Ralph Olliffe, Nintuer was chosen Mayor, where
above the line? was his house, † and what was the ☨?

In what part of Wine S.t was the Elephant al.s the
four storries? and any particulars respecting it —

29. WILLIAM TYSON
Queries about Bristol inns.
(Bris. L., Jefferies Coll.)

Oh ye odd Ringing & Tolling for
upon Tollings at 7. 10 x 2
are relics of by gone days.
When I came & so understood
Here the Sermon Bell is
seven ore [one?] before Service
then Set - Pulled off & rung
out - at the half hour, Pulled
at the Quarter - there Chimes
for ten minutes - & if a 6th
Athy no Passing Bell
Sung Pray - That is our
Use. & very intelligible &c —

Vineyard Sexton & Sexton
the Passing Bell is Tolled
& rung out as soon as
possible after death —
are now altogether
Tolled Bell for children,
until 4 & 3 × 2 × 2 full
set - then the age —
At the Funeral. a Tolling
and Roll an hour - not
Rolling or ring up —
then Chime Slowly into
Church - Toiling an
Crime

30. HENRY THOMAS ELLACOMBE
from a letter on bell-ringing customs, 1875
(G.R.O., P.217 CW 4/13)

31. SAMUEL ROFFEY MAITLAND
The quarrel between Bishop Miles Smith and Dean Laud
(Glos. Coll. 2091)

Broad(?)
17 Feb. 1834

Dear Sir

(1) your have been offered 20£ Guineas (...)
justice to both yourself & the Govt. not to afford it
suppose to give you less than 25£. But Govt.
more ever left you here is left of our claim...

32. SIR THOMAS PHILLIPPS, Bt.
Draft reply to letter from G.W. Counsel (Illustration no. 18)
(Bodl. MS. Phillipps-Robinson, c.451, fol.108)

"a piece of glass, nicknamed the diamond, of great value supposed to represent rubies & diamonds" which the village Cicerone rejects from the bookseller's authority is every admiring visitor called Judas! On inspection holes (concave) & lines are ground into a ruby-stained bit of glass, the beauty of which like the pink of woman's cheek is but skin deep. thus a white surface is exposed to as most ingeniously to represent precious stones in a jewel fastening the outer robe which opens on the thigh discovering an under-dress hose & shoes.

The same method is adopted as regards
1. a brooch fastening Solomon's ermine tippet
2. a jewel fastening the upper part of a woman's dress } same window
3. Judgment of David- top of a red turban with white spots {St. aid to winds.
4) 1 W. fr. y W. 1st light girdle round y. waist & hanging down
    2 yellow roses introduced
    4th lighter strips sustaining hose

well worth preservation but I have no room for them, for my house is over-full of books.

I have not heard any thing further about the Casket & have not been to Somerset House since you were here. I will call in a day or two & make Inquiry —

Any body may become a Member of the Institute who chooses to pay the annual subscription — It is not an Elective body like the Antiquaries and, of course, carries no credit with it. The 30 guineas at the Antiquaries would make you a Fellow for life & it is much the best thing for a young man to pay the life subscription. I was about 45 when I was elected, and now wish I had paid the life subsⁿ. — I have paid already nearly half as much again.

Lady Maclean & Blanche send kind regards. The latter says she knows you mean to forget all about the Photographs but she does not

34. SIR JOHN MACLEAN
(Part of) letter to the Rev. W. Jago, 1871, on the Society of Antiquaries etc.
(Brooks Coll., R. Institution of Cornwall)

they had felt in my statement of the case. For example – the Rev. Isaac Taylor said that he had found it "as interesting as a novel". I think therefore that I could abridge and popularize the main argument and facts so that it would be entertaining to a cultivated audience

Ja~ Gentlemen
your ob.t Serv.t
Thomas Kerslake

35. THOMAS KERSLAKE
(Part of) letter to the Council of the Bristol Museum & Library
(Bris. L., B26069)

The present Christian Unitarian Society at Cheltenham was established August 1832. This was effected by Mr. Foster in his own dwelling house, who at that period had recently settled here from Bath. Unitarian Worship was regularly celebrated every Sabbath for three years by Mr. Foster in his residence. The worshippers next removed to the Mechanics Institution, which was opened for public worship by the Rev. G. Brock, then of Glouc. on March 22, 1835. For nearly two years the Society rented this room, when an opportunity offering itself, they removed to the Friends Meeting House, in Manchester Place. This, the oldest Dissenting Chapel in the town, was formally opened for Unitarian Worship by the Rev. T. Davis, of Evesham, on June 25, 1837. The

36. JOHN GODING

From the transactions of the Cheltenham Unitarian Congregation, 1844

1º Elizabethæ. A general pardon to Thomas Dutton of Sherborne Esq, called Thomas Dutton als Clifforde oℓm

of treason whilhom conspiring homicide felonyes, Vary ortrayn acceʃʃary to the same misprisions Violorum petitions Carnikelds, Confederacy notʃ rowts hospiteſ, escapes, Extortions Reʃpexned in all of parton howevere, felony or Treason – Mortened linnants escheting fyrnis fryments Debts – Tempering with Debts, Recogc. &c – offuch rents paines fnn – Stoneses of death – And of all fuch forfs. fines aletement due to the Crown through Extortion – of all Attaintes attaintores Symns & Payris – full wrongly e meanes

518. Gambado's (Geoffrey) Annals of Horsemen-
-ship. 8vo. Bath. 1792.

519. Kidder's (Robt-Bp.) Shrines and useful-
-Chees of the Old and New World. 2 vols
8vo. Lond. 1851.

520. Lanes (Theo.) Students Guide through Lin-
-colns Inn. Sm. 8vo. Lond. 1823.

521. [Nares' (Edw.)] Heraldic Anomalies. 2
vols Sm. 8vo. Lond. 1824.

522. Catalogue of the Manuscripts in the
possession of the Earl of Hardwicke.
Privately printed. 4to. 1794.

38. BEAVER HENRY BLACKER
From the catalogue of his library
(Glos. Coll. 12412, p.114)

Shewing the great satisfaction of knowing that my educational efforts, during the last fourteen years, in his Parish, have been accomplished a large amount of good — in all which I thankfully own the kind sympathy and confidence you my dear Sir have at all times been pleased to extend to

Yours most faithfully
H L Nicholls

39. HENRY GEORGE NICHOLLS
(Part of) letter to the Office of Works concerning Holy Trinity School, Drybrook, 1862 (P.R.O., F3/209)

The manuscripts, books, maps &c described in this list were bequeathed to the Museum and Library by the Rev. H. T. Ellacombe, the historian of Bitton, and were received from his executors in the autumn of 1885. After being examined by the late John Maclean, the boxes were consigned to the cellar underneath the Lecture Room, where they remained until the institution was transferred to the Corporation. A portion of the documents had then perished owing to the dampness of their place of deposit. The remaining loose papers were arranged in fifteen large volumes in 1894-5. (See Pos. 772 to 784).

J.Latimer

40. JOHN LATIMER
Note on the Rev. H.T. Ellacombe's MSS
(Bris. L., B28264)

College Green
Gloucester
April 17th
1854

My dear Sir,

I send you a rather rough account of my late researches; next month I hope to have much more for you on. I have quite relics enough in my reach to make a very nice etching from. If you think it worth your while I can work on some subject of [...]

41. JOHN RANDALL CLARKE
(Part of) letter to J.G. Nicholls on Roman finds in Gloucester, 1854.
(Fitzwilliam Museum, Cambridge, MS Perceval, L57)

As the victim of my position I am obliged to throw myself upon your indulgence to allow me to accept the conditions of the Free Libraries Committee in respect to the time that they appoint me to take duty under their authority. They meet tomorrow (Friday) & should the interval to be then assigned seem brief, I would of suffered to leave at short notice, be not forgetful of the duty still incumbent on me of assisting my successor to the utmost of my power in all that respects the arrangements of the Museum Library, with deep acknowledgments I am, Gentlemen Your dutiful servant John Taylor
Librarian

£30, being balance of £50, paid to Mr Strong
by H H H Lettres 6/9, in 1043, for my
"use & ornament"; W.S. should have taught
me his trade, but up to his death I
was left hand to clean windows & run errands
up & down in the shop —
those who have not had the care
of an orphan man Harry Harte —
near Harry Harte

Nov 30/77

W. S. G G

This book contains the translation made for me by Mr. E. M. Thompson of the British Museum (5th May 1878) of a collection of original Bristol documents then in my possession which had been sold at Mr. Tyson's sale in 1851, and were purchased by the Revd. Thos. Maddox who had them arranged mounted and bound at the British Museum —

Francis F. Fox.

Visit to Coberley Dec: 9: 1878.

On Monday Dec. 9: 1878 I went by train from Gloucester to Cheltenham & after having had lunch with Mr? Douglas & Mr? Sandys I walked via Charlton Park, Sandy Lane & Cockhampton with & Mr? Wilson, the Rectory, Coberley. I was immediately struck on entering the house by the large quantity of valuable oak furniture, most of it, at the seat of Cumberland manufacture but some of earlier date? a table in the Study of hands with 'linch worth' carving from Whitley Church — In the evening I adjourned the parishioners on the subject of the Conquest of India & Mirais worth here copy? in Turkey.

The next morning, Tuesday Dec.10th I examined the parish registers & noted many entries of interest relating — to the Bridges family, notably the baptism of Skyselmar & deaths of Giles, Lord Chandos — & the 'Castleman family' notably an account of Mr. Castleman's disaster in connexion with the Lords & Kettle — & the Rectors of Coberley, notably testatives who died in 1651 aet: 105, & some families (in modern 1456/89 — He next paid a visit to the Church which is almost a new one, having been rebuilt 7 years since — the original tower remained with the Bordered? arch on NW & SW — a pew which ? — & the Church's tradition ? Thomas de Berkeley 14 Edw. III (see Pat) 1346 had been rebuilt with same notes — all the rest is totally new —

Books purchased by me
relating to Gloucestershire.

Berkeley M.S.   3   3
Transactions of Glos Arch¹ Soc¹y
   8 vols & binding   6 14
Glos Notes & Queries 2 vol things 2 7 6
Storer Delineations of Glos   2   6
Dents Sudeley & Winchcomb   1 13
Blunts Tewkesbury Abbey   2   2
Annals of Chepstow Castle   1   6
Lysons Antiquities of Glos   2 10
Fennicks Visitations 1683   1   1
Bigland Reprint of pt 1   1   1 6
~~Pooleys Glos Coffers~~   9 6
Lees Hist. of Tetbury   12 6
Thornbury Castle   4 6
Marshalls Glos col 2 & binding   5
Nucleus Hist. Cirencester   5
Lyders Hist. Tewkesbury   10

'Also the book of notes, the places with the St. deeds. Prebendary Pickenden's list is no doubt still at the Church. It is a most interesting Collection of Documents; it will have been that the Scrivenship 1 Prewer Short can be traced back without a break for 543 years, and it, are 630 years ago is known. St Thomas's can fairly claim to be one of the oldest Parents/Parishes even in Bristol. I am still interested in the Old Church, and am always glad to hear how it is prospering.

Yours sincerely, Charles D. Taylor.

47. CHARLES SAMUEL TAYLOR
From a letter about early deeds of his former church, St. Thomas's, Bristol, 1924
(B.R.O., P/St. T., HM/17)

Dear Sir —

I enclose you rect. Very sorry we had not a note of your change of address. I have had it altered.

Do you think that you cd help under Vol XIII of Glos. Reg. which I am now printing. I am badly in want of Copy. Could you not contribute Minsterworth Marr. Registers?

Yours [truly]
W. P. W. Phillimore

Rev C. O. Bartlett

---

48. WILLIAM PHILLIMORE WATTS PHILLIMORE
Letter to the Vicar of Minsterworth, 1907
(Inserted in G.R.O. copy of Phillimore's *Glos. Marriage Registers*, Vol. I)

In the same court, John Brownsmyth sued for performance of an alleged contract of matrimony. He alleged that she had said she was content to take him as husband, provided he obtained the good will of Mr Clifford, her landlord, whereupon he was ordered to produce Mr Clifford in the court; this he apparently failed to do & the sentence of Bishop Hooper was, that there was no contract & the widow was free to marry whom she would.

For blasphemy, Thomas Mayle was sentenced by the bishop, to learn the ten commandments of God by heart not later than before the next festival of All Saints, on which day

49. FRANK STEP HOCKADAY
From his abstracts of Gloucester Consistory Court (1551) for Frampton-on-Severn.
(Glos. Coll. Hockaday Abstracts)

"really" "Middle-ham"   a Villa lies behind it on
                        upper field corner!
Mill-ham-pool Farm   many 2nd G. silver coins
         ? grave-yard   May. 6. '08

There is more digging, and I come upon
some fresh RBr. rims + bases
The recurrence of animal remains here.
Such as cattle-bones (frequent) seems to
suggest that the ancient burial place (R.Br)
of a "Villa" lies, later, served for a farm of oxen
+ cows, or else their cemetery during a murrain
on the property. An R.B. Villa was no doubt in the
next field N.   early
have been found + photographed. Only two skulls
I gave slides of these to
                            Sir Arthur Keith (1921)

Broadway with its bended up-hill great road
+ grey-gold cables against the woodlands above
yet with memories of old unhappy far-off things
+ battle, long-ago: + fleeing Lancastrians
at Didbrook.

50. WELBORE ST. CLAIR BADDELEY
Romans and romance: from a notebook, 1908
(Glos. Coll., Baddeley 90, fol. 45d)

51. WILLIAM HENRY KNOWLES
Sketch of Saxon work in Jarrow church, Co. Durham, 1898.
(B.L., Add. 37508, f.112)

52. ROLAND AUSTIN
From a letter to Wilfrid Leighton, 1 April 1943, referring to Bristol war damage and the Theatre Royal, Bristol.
(in possession of Mr. Gerard Leighton, 1979)

Index

Place-names, where no county is stated, are in Gloucestershire. Other English place-names are arranged under counties.

Adams, Daniel, 42
  William, 18, 22, 34, 41–2, 124, 148–9
Adlestrop, 50
Aerio Mastix, 43–4
Agas, Ralph, 17
Alderley, 68
Aldrich, Henry, 32
Ames, Joseph, 62
Annalia Dubrensia, 62
antiquaries, antecedents of, 17–19
  as artists, 35, 64, 79, 97, 103–04, 109, 120, 125,
  female, 15
  pseudonyms of, 31, 99, 100*n*, 103, 116, 123
  societies of, *see* societies, antiquarian
Antiquaries, Elizabethan Society of, 21
Antiquaries of London, Society of, 15, 21, 24, 57, 77, 79, 80, 81*n*, 171, 181
Antiquity, 137
Ap Adam family, 97
Archaeological Handbook of Gloucestershire, 26
Archaeological Institute, Royal, 96, 99, 110, 120
Archard, William, 38–9
Ariconium, 88
Asteria columnaris, 161
Atkyns, Sir Edward, sen., 49
  Sir Edward, jun., 49
  Edward, 51
  family, 51
  Sir Robert, sen., 49, 51
  Sir Robert, jun., 20, 22, 23, 45, 47, 48*n*, 49–52, 53, 67, 72, 87, 154
Aubrey, John, 23
Austin, Roland, 27–8, 51, 52, 68, 88, 90, 131–2, 137–8, 199

Bacon, Nathaniel, 35*n*
Baddeley, W. St. Clair, 27, 133–4, 197
Ballard, George, 20*n*, 21, 53, 57–8, 62–3, 159
  John, 62
Barkham, John, 15*n*

Barratt, Dr. D. M., 44*n*
Barrett, William, 21, 22, 70–71, 74, 91, 94, 119, 162
  Rev. W. T., 71
Bathurst, Allen, 1st Earl, 67
  Charles Bragge, 161, 166
  family, of Lydney, 68
Beachley peninsula, 96, 174
Bedfordshire, antiquities in, 88
Belas Knap long barrow, 26
Bellows, John, 15, 120
bells, church, and bell-ringing, 24, 101, 177
Bennett, James, 24, 98, 175
Berkeley family, 19, 36–9, 80, 81*n*
  Henry, 17th Lord, 36–7
  Maurice, 8th Lord, 39
  Thomas, 36
Berkeley, Breadstone in, 167
  Castle, 36–8
  Hundred & Liberty of, 36–7
  Manuscripts, 27, 36–9, 88–9, 110
  muniments, 38–9
  Plantation, *see* Virginia
Berkshire, antiquities in, 88
  Reading, 53, 137
Best family, 83
  Martha, 83
Beverstone, 97
Bibliographer's Manual of Gloucestershire Literature, 16, 27, 125, 127, 137
Bigland, family, 66
  Ralph, 22, 23, 43, 53, 56*n*, 64–6, 82, 87, 105–6, 160
  Sir Ralph, 65
  Richard, 64, 84*n*
Bisley, 15
Bitton, 24, 38, 101–02
  Barr's Court, 102
  Court Farm, 102
Blacker, Beaver H., 25, 38, 116, 130, 185
  Latham, 116*n*
Blatchly, Dr. J. M., 15
Blore, Edward, 164

Bodleian Library, Oxford, 20, 21, 44, 45–6, 47–8, 51, 56, 57–8, 60–61, 62–3, 66, 68, 75–6, 97, 106, 150–3, 156, 159, 165, 179
Boke of Noblesse, 32
Boone (bookseller), 89
Bosworth, Battle of, 145
Botoner, Elizabeth, 31
  family, 31
  William, *see* Worcestre, William
Bourton-on-the-Water, 114
Braikenridge, George W., 24, 42, 71, 91–2, 100n, 168, 171
  and Honeywill, merchants, 91
  family, 91
  'Gothic' library of, 91, 121, 168
Bazeley family, 125–6
  Canon William, 27, 73n, 115, 125–6, 192
Branwhite, Nathan, 74
Brickdale, Matthew, 18
Brimscombe, 82
Bristol, 17–19, 22–23, 25, 31–2, 70, 89
  Abbey, 21
  All Saints' church, 34
  Art Gallery, 91–2, 100
  Ashton Court, 71
  Backs, 145, 149
  booksellers, 111, 123
  Canynge's Place, 122
  Cathedral, 21
  charters, 74, 119
  chronicles (MS.), 18, 41
  churches, 84n, 129
  Diocesan archives, 131–2
  flood at, 145
  gilds, 124
  Grammar School, 74
  Guilder's Inn, 122
  historians of, 18–19, 22–3, 34–5, 41, 45–6, 70–71, 74, 82–3, 94, 99, 119, 122,
  inns, 176
  Kalendars' Gild, 34, 35n
  Kingrode, 145
  Library, City, 27, 74, 91–2, 95n, 100, 101–2, 119, 122, 168, 171, 182, 187, 189
  Library Society, 122, 187
  Little Red Book of, 34
  Mayor's Kalendar, 34–5, 144
  Merchant Venturers, 119, 124
  municipal constitutions of, 122
  plans and surveys of, 18, 31–2, 35, 123

  port, 17
  Record Office and City Archives, 35, 42, 71, 74, 91, 100, 119, 124, 129, 144, 148, 162, 164, 191, 194
  riots, 123
  Royal Fort School, 74
  St. Mary Redcliffe church, 71, 94, 129
  St Michael's church, 74
  St Thomas the Martyr church, 129, 194
  ship 'Anthony' of, 145
  shooting-match at (1616), 148–9
  Theatre, 199
  topography, 31–2, 35, 71, 74, 91–2
  Town Clerks of, 18, 34–5
  William Worcestre's survey of, 18, 31–2
Bristol & Gloucestershire Archaeological Society, 16, 25–8, 61, 106, 110, 114, 119, 122–5, 129, 135, 137
Bristol Memorialist, 99–100, 173
Bristol Mercury, 119
Bristol Times & Mirror 22, 99–100, 123
British Archaeological Association, 26, 122
British (Museum) Library, 32, 38–9, 43–4, 49–50, 56, 78, 80, 83, 101–02, 106, 114, 170, 175, 198
British Magazine, 103
British Record Society, 130
Britton, John, 24, 76, 87, 99, 171
Broadwell, 50
Brock, Rev. G., 183
Brockworth, 19, 43–4
  see also Cooper's Hill
Brompton, Richard, 65
Brookthorpe, 103
Brunel, M.I., 101
Bruton, H. W., 80
Brydges, Annabella, 50
  family, 192
  Hon. & Rev. Henry, 50
Buckingham, Henry, Duke of, 145
Buckland, 105
Busby's Latin Grammar, 67
Bute, 1st Marquess of, 82

Calcot Barn, 80
Cam, 130
Cambridge, Fitzwilliam Museum, 121n, 188
Cambridge University, Colleges of:
  Corpus Christi, 32

Trinity, 103, 117
Trinity Hall, 127
Camden, William, 17, 77
Camden Society, 110
canals, 117
Carew, Richard, 17
Carter, John, 81*n*
cartularies:
  Cirencester Abbey, 54–5
  Flaxley Abbey, 106
  Gloucester Abbey, 54–5
  Winchcombe Abbey, 25, 54–5, 114–5
Castleman family, 192
Catcot(t), Rev. George, 161–2
Cerney, North, 153
  Calmsden in, 153
  Common Fields, 153
  Woodmancote in, 153
Chandos, 8th Lord, 50
Charlett, Dr. Arthur, 62
Charlton Kings, 53–6, 116
  Charlton Park, 53
  Manor of Ashley, 53
Chatterton, Thomas, 70
Chavenage House and chapel, 23, 185
Chedworth, Lord, 62
Chedworth Roman villa, 26
Chelt, River, 155
Cheltenham, 25, 88–9, 90*n*, 112–13, 116, 135
  Friends' Meeting House, 183
  historians of, 112
  Library, 113
  Manor and court books, 53, 55, 155
  Mechanics' Institution, 183
  notes on history of, 55, 155
  parish church, 56*n*, 155
  poll book, 55
  Thirlestane House, 25, 105
  unitarian Congregation, 112-3, 183
Cheltenham Examiner, 112–3
Cheltenham Free Press, 112
Cheshire,
  Chester, King's School, 96
  manuscript material for, 96–7
  Ormerod's History of, 96
Chipping Campden, 21, 62
  Grammar School, 57
  notes for history of, 62
Chipping Sodbury, 124
Cholmondeley, Reginald, 38–9
Cirencester, 22, 31, 54, 67–9, 140–1
  Abbey cartulary, 54–5
  church, 68, 80, 141

George Inn, 151
Grammar School, 82
historians of, 68, 133
Civil War, 36, 38, 43, 127
Clarke, John Randall, 120–21, 188
  F.W., 120
  Joseph, 120
Clifford, Major A.W., 85
  Mrs E.M., 27, 28
  family, of Frampton-on-Severn, 170, 196
  Nathaniel, 170
Clifford's Inn, 53
Clifton, 25, 94, 110, 116, 122
  Antiquarian Club, 111, 119, 122
Clinton family, 88, 90
clocks, care of, 147
Clutterbuck family, 170
Coaley ('Cowley'), 69*n*
Coates, 51, 141
Coberley, 192
Colby, Rev. Jonathan, 47
Cole, William, 52
Coleford, 110, 118
Collectanea Glocestriensia, 85
collectors of antiquities, books and MSS., 21, 24, 25, 43, 62, 85, 91, 99, 105–07, 108, 114–5, 124, 127, 161
Cooke, J.H., 36
Cooper's Hill, in Brockworth, 19, 43–4, 151
Corbet, John, 75
Cornwall, 25, 110
  Blisland, 110
  Royal Institution of, 110
  St. Ives, 125
  St. Michael's Mount, 31
Corry, John, 94, 95*n*
Cotswold, 'derivation' of, 141
Cotteswold Naturalists' Field Club, 25–7, 108, 137
Counsel, Anne, 75
  George W., 24, 61, 75–6, 165, 179
  Joshua, 75
Crawford, O.G.S., 137
Creswick family, 102*n*
Crisp, F.A. 39
Croome, W.I., 28, 128
——, of Breadstone, 167
Crown Forests, records of, 118
Cunnington, William, 23 and *n*

Dallaway family, 82–3
  Rev. James, 23, 32, 64, 82–4, 92*n*, 168

James, sen., 82
William, 82
Dance, George, jun., 80
Davies, William, 89
Davis, Rev. T., 183
Dean, Forest of, 25, 96, 117–8
　churches and schools in, 117
　historians of, 117
　iron industry, 118, 161
Deerhurst church, 135
Delafield family, 86
Devon, church bells of, 101
　Clyst St. George, 101
　Exeter, 25
　Exeter v. Bristol shooting-match, 148–9
Dobson-Hinton, Dr. D.P., 27, 28
Dobyns-Yate, Rev. H.G., 22n, 160
Domesday Survey of Gloucestershire, 27, 129
Doynton, 59
Driffield, 47
Drybrook, 117–8, 186
Ducarel, A.C., 47–8, 60, 71, and n
Dugdale, Sir William, 17, 36–7
Duntisbourne Rous, Pinbury Park, 49–50
Durham, 119
　Jarrow church, 198
Dursley, 85–6
Dutton, Thomas of Sherborne, 184
Dyde, William, 98

Edinburgh and Leith, inscriptions from, 66n
effigies in churches, 15
Elkstone, Combend Farm in, 80
Ellacombe, Rev. Henry T., 24, 100n, 101–02, 114, 119, 177, 187
Elrington, C.R., 52n, 98
Elstob, Elizabeth, 62
Elton family, 91
Essays in Bristol and Gloucestershire History, 25n and *passim*
Essex, Birchanger, 47
Estlin, Rev. Dr., 91, 94
Evans, Dame Joan, 15 and n, 21n, 28, 81 and ns
　Rev. John (Anglican), 94
　Rev. John (Presbyterian and historian), 22, 94–5, 99, 100n, 173
　John (printer), 92, 94, 95n
excavation, 23, 26–7, 79–80, 120–21, 133, 135, 197

Fairfax, Lord, 151
Fairford, 68, 108, 180
Falfield, 98
Fastolf, Sir John, 31, 36, 143
Field family, of Paganhill, 85n
Filton, 74
Finberg, H.P.R., 28, 62
Fisher, Benjamin, 93
　Paul Hawkins, 24, 93, 172
　Samuel, 93
Flaxley Abbey cartulary, 106
Fleming, Lindsay, 78, 83, 84n, 138
Folger Shakespeare Library, U.S.A., 61
Forest of Dean, *see* Dean
Forster, R.H., 135
Fosbroke, Thomas Dudley, 23, 36, 45, 54, 60, 64–5, 75–6, 87–90, 170
Fosbrooke family, 90
　William, 87
Foss Way, 141
Fox, Francis F., 25, 42, 119, 124, 191
　Dr. F.K., 124
Frampton-on-Severn, 72, 196
Franks, Sir A.W., 80
Frith, Brian, 46, 61n, 73n
Frocester Court, 64
Fry, Dr., 26
G.S., 130
Furber, Rev. ——, 183
Furney, James, Mayor of Gloucester, 59
　Archdeacon Richard, 21, 45, 59 61, 68, 87, 131, 158
Fust, Sir Francis, Bt., 38

Gardner, Ann (aft. Counsel), 75
　Clement S.B., 83
　David, 75
　family records, 83
　Sankey, 83
　Sophia, 83
Gentleman's Magazine, *passim*
George, William, 25, 88, 111, 116, 122, 123, 190
Gladstone, W.E., 104n
glass, stained, 80, 180
Gloucester, Robert of, 17 and n, 157
Gloucester, 17, 19, 60, 75, 83
　Abbey (St Peter's), 17, 21, 54, 55
　archaeological finds in, 120–21, 135, 188
　architectural history of, 120
　'As sure as God's at', 158
　Blackfriars, 135
　Chapter Library, 55

Christ Church parish, 103
City archives, 54, 59, 61
City Library, 27, 39, 68, 85, 127, 137–8; *see also* Gloucestershire Collection
City Museum, 120
Consistory Court, 131–2
Crypt School, 59, 137
Diocesan and Dean & Chapter archives, 27, 54, 61, 131–2
historians of, 23–4, 45–6, 59–60, 67–8, 72–3, 75–6, 87–90, 127
King's (Cathedral or College) School, 72, 75, 93
Literary & Scientific Institution, 109, 120–21
Longsmith Street, 121
Newark House, 76
notes on, 55, 158
Probate Registry and records, 106, 130, 131
Ram Inn, 158
Roman Research Committee, 135
St. John's church, 20, 45
St. Mary de Crypt church, 60, 167 (font)
St. Mary de Lode church, 72, 75
St. Michael's church, 59–60, 72, 163
topography of 55, 89
Westgate Street (Tudor carvings in no. 163), 125
Gloucester–Berkeley canal, 117
Gloucester Journal, 98, 137
Gloucestershire:
 agriculture, 72–3
 antiquarian societies, *see* societies
 archaeology in 23, 26, 79–80
 architecture, medieval, 135
 church bells, 101–02
 churches, 65, 80, 121
 County Library, 137
 County Records, catalogue of, 127
 historians of, 20–21, 23, 44, 45–6, 47–8, 49–52, 53, 60–61, 64–6, 67–9, 72–3, 87–90
 Inquisitions Post Mortem, 130
 Lieutenancy minutes, 38
 place–names, 37, 133
 Pleas of the Crown(A.D.1221), 104
 poll book (1734), 55
 Visitations (Heralds'), 106, 110
Gloucestershire Collection (Gloucester City Library),
 Catalogue of the, 16, 137
 MS. material in, *passim*

Gloucestershire Record Office, 27, 38, 127, 137
 MS. material in, *passim*
Gloucestershire Notes & Queries, 25, 116, 130, and references *passim*
Gloucestershire Repository, The, 93
Goding, John, 25, 112–3, 183
Gracie, Captain H.S., R.N., 28
Graves, family and pedigree, 57, 58n
 Morgan, 58
 Richard, sen., 21, 57–8, 62, 156–7, 159
 Richard, jun., 57
 Samuel, 57
Graves-Hamilton, Miss, 58
 Sidney, 58n
Guillim, John, 15
Guise, Sir William, Bt., 26, 106

Hadrian's Wall, 135
Hale, Matthew, 68
Halliwell (aft. Halliwell-Phillipps), J.O., 106
Hampshire, Cheriton, 59
 Houghton, 59
 Southampton, 31
Hardwicke, MSS. of Earl of, 185
Haresfield, 72–3
 Court, 108
Harford, Rev. F.K., 42
 Joseph, 42
Harleian Society, 110
Hart, Anne, 43
 Dr. Cyril, 117–8
 Mrs. Gwen, 55, 112–3
 Richard, Prior of Llanthony, 43
Harvey, Dr. John, 19, 32, 141
Hasted, Edward, 20
Hayles, 67
 Abbey, 67, 133
Hearne, Thomas, 21, 57, 59–61, 62, 156, 159
Hempstead Court, 77
Heralds and heraldry, 15, 17, 22, 46, 55, 64–6, 82, 88, 106, 108–09, 110, 125, 168, 169, 185
Herbert, Dr. N.M., 68–9, 93
Hereford Diocese, 72
Herefordshire, antiquities in, 88
 Ross-on-Wye, 88
 Walford, 88
Hertfordshire, Monken Hadley, 49
 St. Albans, 58
Hetty Pegler's Tump (in Uley), 26
Higford, John, 76

Hill Court (in Hill), 38
historians, county, 17
Hoare, Sir R. Colt, 23
Hobson family (Bristol), 122
Hockaday Abstracts, The, 131–2
Hockaday, Frank S., 27, 131–2, 196
Holbrow family, 130
Holme, Randle, 96
Hooper, John, Bishop of Gloucester, 75, 196
Horfield, 74
Horsley, 85, 87
Howe, J. Grubham, M.P., 54, 56n
Hucclecote, 59
Huddleston, C. Roy, 94–5
Hughes, Robert, 87, 89
Hunt, Dodington, 54–5
 William H. (aft. Prynne), 55
Hunter, Joseph, 83
Hyett, Benjamin, 60
 Sir Francis A., 27, 60, 125, 127–8, 137, 193
 W.H. 93, 127

Icomb, 114
Index Library, 130
Inventories, probate, 132
Ireland, 25, 116, 149
iron industry, 117–8
Irvine, Sir James, 134

Jacobites, 54
Jago, Rev. W., 181
Jeffries, Charles T., Collections of, 74, 100
Jenkins, Phillip, 41
Jones, John (of Gloucester), 108–09

Kedgwin, Thomas, 41
Kemble, Ewen in, 141
Kendrick, Sir Thomas, 17, 32
Kent, Rochester, 50
Kerslake, Thomas, 25, 111, 182
Kiftsgate Hundred, 57
King, Thomas (of Chepstow), 174
Kingsdown, 94
Kingsholm (Gloucester), 120
Kingswood Forest, 102
Kirby, Isabel, 56n, 132
Knight family, of Slimbridge, 40
 Samuel, 57
Knowles, W.H., 27, 135–6, 198

Lambarde, William, 17
Lambeth Palace Library, 24, 32, 103, 104 and n

lampreys, 143
Lancashire, 64
 genealogical material, 96
 Manchester, 96
Langtoft, Peter, 60
Lansdowne, 1st Marquess of, 58
Latimer, John, 25, 102, 119, 187
Laud (Archbishop), William, Dean of Gloucester, 178
Laverton, 105
Lawrence, Sir Thomas, 77, 79
Lean, Robert, 110
Leckhampton Hill, excavation at, 135
Leicestershire, 36
 Melton Mowbray, 38–9
 Seagrave, 39
Leighton, Gerard, 199
 Wilfrid, 199
Leland, John, 17, 35
Le Neve, Peter, 46, 47–8
Lewis, John, 46
 Samuel, 46
 Wilmarth S., 83
Lindley, E.S. 28, 38–9
Livingstone, Marie C., 92
Llanthony Secunda Abbey, 43, 121
Lloyd–Baker, T.J., 26
Longford, 117
Luttrell family, 123
 H.F., 190
Lydney, 68, 94, 131–2, 161
 Pirton Passage, 161
 The Scowles, 161
Lysons, Rev. Daniel, 23, 77–8, 79, 83, 166
 family, 77, 78, and n, 79–80, 138
 Mr., 51
 Samuel, 23, 26, 79–81, 84n, 166, 167
 Rev. Samuel, sen., 77
 Canon Samuel, 26, 61, 77, 80, 85

McFarlane, K.B., 32, 33n, 143n
Maclean, Sir John, 25, 27, 36, 39, 58n, 110, 181, 187
Macray, William D., 46, 61n
Madden, Sir Frederic, 106
Magna Britannia, 23, 77, 79
Maitland, Frederick W., 24, 103–04
 Samuel Roffey, 24, 103–04, 178
Manning, Owen, 20
manuscripts destroyed by fire, 51, 58
Manuscripts, Royal, 44
Marshall, William, 73
Marshfield, Old Meeting House, 94
Martin, Thomas (of Suffolk), 46, 48
Maskell, Rev. William, 124, 191

Matson, 125–6
Mayle, Thomas, 196
Michigan, University of, 55
Mickleton, 21, 57–8, 157
Middle Hill Press, 54, 64, 105–06
Milham-post Farm, 197
Minchinhampton, 45, 46n
Minsterworth, 15, 195
Moir, Esther, 45, 62
Monmouth's Rebellion, 102
Monmouthshire, Chepstow, 174
   Chepstow Castle, 110
   Piercefield estate (in St. Kingsmark), 174
   Tintern Abbey, 31
Montagu, Lady Mary Wortley, 83
Morant, Philip, 20
Moreyn, Master, 143
Morgan, Alexander, 71
Morse, Robert, 57
Munby, A.N.L., 54, 105–07
Murch, Jerom, 94

Nash, T.R., 20, 57
Nasmith, James, 32, 33n
Nayler, Sir George, 82
Neale, Mrs. F.A., 19, 32, and n
Newent, 20
Newton family, of Bitton, 102
   Francis (artist), 80
New York Public Library, 39
Niblett, Daniel J., 108
   John D.T., 25, 73n, 108–09, 180
Nibley, North, 36
Nicholls, Henry George, 25, 117–8, 186
   Sir George 117–8
Nichols, John, 47, 62
   John Bowyer, 76
   John Gough, 88, 120, 188
   Messrs. (printers and publishers), 23, 65, 90, 175
Nicholson, William, Bishop of Gloucester, 45
Norden, John, 17
Norfolk, 11th Duke of, 82
Norfolk, 31
   Ketteringham, 51
   Norwich, 31–2
   Pockthorpe, 31
   Record Office, 32
Norman, G., 112, 113n
Northumberland, 119, 135
   Corbridge-on-Tyne (Corstopitum), 135

Newcastle-on-Tyne, 25, 27, 119, 135
Northwick, Lord, 105
Norton, John, 61
Notes & Queries, 25, 101, 103, 116
   references to, *passim*
Nottingham, 130
   University, Dept. of MSS., 90
Nourse, Timothy, 19–20
   Walter (d. 1699), 20
   Walter (d. 1711), 20
Nympsfield long barrow, 26

Offa's Dyke, 96
Oldys, William, 51
O'Neill, Hugh, 91, 92n
Ormerod, Eleanor, 96–7
   family, 96–7
   George, 24, 96–7, 100n, 169, 174
   P.J., 96
   Sarah, 97
Osburne, John ('Town Monk' of Gloucester), 158
Oxenton, 142–3
Oxford antiquaries, *see* Ballard, G.; Hearne, T.; Rawlinson, R.; Wood, A.
Oxfordshire, Bigland's collections for, 65
North Oxfordshire Archaeological Society, 114
Oxford, 31
Oxford University, Bodleian Library, *see* Bodleian
   Colleges of:
   Brasenose, 96
   Christ Church, 114
   Corpus Christi, 74
   Great Hart Hall, 31
   Magdalen, 19, 32, 36, 43, 62
   Merton, 72
   New College, 47
   Oriel, 56, 59, 85
   Pembroke, 57, 87
   St. Edmund Hall, 49
   Trinity, 82
   University, 19, 44, 62, 105

Painswick, 127–8
   Castle Hale, 132–3
   church, 133
   House, 127, 137
   Ifold Roman villa, 133
   manor, 133
Panton, Rev. ——, 85
Paris, Matthew, 34

parish registers, 130, 132
Parkman, H.S. 100
Parsons, Richard, 20, 45, 47–8, 50, 153
  Dr. William, 47
Paston letters, 31–2
Peel, Sir Robert, 117
Petter, William, 74
Phelps, John Delafield, 24, 84, 85–6, 169
  J.D., sen., 85
  Sophia, 169
  William, 85
Phillimore family, 130
  Dr. W.P., 130
  W.P.W., 27, 116, 130, 195
Phillipps, Thomas, sen., 105
  Sir Thomas, Bt., 24–5, 64, 75–6, 89, 105–07, 165, 179, and *passim*
Pinbury Park, 49–50
Pitt, John (father, son, grandson), of Stroud, 172
Poor Law and poor relief, 117
Population statistics, 50
Poyntz family, 110
Prinknash Park, 125
Prinn, Ann, 54
  Elizabeth, 54
  John, 20 and *n*, 21, 53–6, 155
  Rev. John, 54, 56*n*
  William, 54
  see also Prynne
Prowse, George Bragge (aft. Prynne), 55
Prynne, William (puritan pamphleteer), 53
  William (of Cheltenham), 56*n*
  William Hunt, 55
  see also Prinn
pseudonyms of antiquaries, *see* antiquaries
Public Records, Royal Commission on, 132
  Samuel Lysons as Keeper of, 79
Public Record Office, 118

Quenington church, 80

Raikes, Robert, 93
Raleigh, Sir Walter, 149
Ralph, Miss Elizabeth, 22*n*, 25*n*, 35, 126, 129
Rawlins, Thomas, 62
Rawlinson, Richard, 48, 58*n*
Rhodes, J.F., 121
Ricart, Philip, 34

Robert, 18, 34–5, 144–5
Richards, Mrs. M., 59, 61*n*
Richmond, Henry, Earl of (Henry VII), 45
Ripley, Peter 88
Robert of Gloucester, *see* Gloucester
Rodborough, 82, 84
Rodmarton, 23, 77
Rogers, Rev. Richard, 60, 68
  Rev. Samuel, 60
  T.D., 76
Roman coins, 159, 197
Romano-British archaeology, 23, 26–7, 79–81, 96, 120–1, 133, 135, 153, 188, 197
Roper, Ida, 15
Roxburghe Club, 85
Royce, David, 25, 26, 114–5, 125, 184
  Matthew, 114
Ruardean, 88–9
Rudd, Mary, 15
Rudder family (formerly Rutter), 67
  Major L.J.V., 68
  Samuel, 20, 22, 23, 60, 67–9, 72, 137, 160, 161, 170
  Samuel, jun., 68
Rudge, Rev. James, D.D., 72
  Archdeacon Thomas, 23, 72–3, 75, 87, 163
  Thomas, sen., 72
Rugby School, 105, 117, 129
Russell, Sir David, 134
Rutland, Oakham, 114
Rutter, Roger, 67

St. Andrews University, 133–4
St. Paul's School, 87
Salisbury, Miss E., 42
Sancroft, Archbishop William, 47
Sanders, G.T. St. J, 93
Sandys, Samuel, 42
Sapperton, 49, 51
savings banks, 117
Saxton, Christopher, 17
Scott, Robert (bookseller), 44
Sedbury Park, in Tidenham, 96, 97*n*
Selwyn family, 126
Severn fisheries, 37
Sewell, E.C., 51
Seyer, Rev. Samuel, 18, 20 and *n*, 22, 35, 42, 71, 74, 164
  Rev. Samuel, sen., 74
Seymour of Sudeley, Lord, 110
Sherborne, Lord, 38
Shipton Oliffe and Sollars, 56*n*

Shipway genealogy case, 130
Shirehampton church, 74
Shropshire, Condover Hall, 38–9
  Shrewsbury School, 124
  Stokesay Court, 55
sickness, the sweating, 145
Slimbridge, 40
Smith, Brian S., 46–8, 51, 52*n*
  family, of Ashton Court, Bristol, 71
  family, of N. Nibley, and descendants, 38–9
  John ('of Nibley'), 19, 27, 35, 36–40, 89, 146–7
  Lucy Toulmin, 35
  Miles, Bishop of Gloucester, 104, 178
Smith-Pigott sale, 38, 66
Smythe (and Smythe-Owen) family, 38
  Nicholas, 39
societies, antiquarian, 21–2, 25–8, 108
  see also Antiquaries of London, Society of; Bristol & Gloucestershire Archaeological Society; Cotteswold Naturalists' Field Club; Gloucestershire Archaeological Society (*c* 1840)
Sodbury, Chipping and Old, 124
Somerford (?Keynes), 50
Somerset, 91, 101
  Archaeological Society, 99, 111
  Banwell, 129
  Bath Grammar School, 77, 79
  Bath Roman Baths, 135
  Brislington, 91, 124
  Brockley Hall, 38, 66
  church bells of, 101
  Clevedon, 91, 111
  Collinson's History of, 91
  Dunster, 25, 123
  Glastonbury, 31
  High Ham, 71
  Swanswick, 56*n*
  Wells, 31
  Wraxall, 71
Sopwith, Thomas, 118
Speed, John, 17, 44
Spiritual Quixote, The, 57
Stanford, Thomas, MSS. of, 84
Steer, F.W., 84 and *n*
Stephens, monument of Thomas, in Stroud church, 172
Stone, Mr. Daw's school at, 98
Stow, John, 17
Stow-on-the-Wold, 114–5
Strong, William, 88, 123, 190

Stroud, 75, 82, 116
  Field Place, 85
  parish church, 172
  The Castle, 93
Stroud Journal, 93, 116
Strype, John, 104
Stukeley, William, 23, 158
Sunday schools, 93
Surrey, Archdeacon of, *see* Furney, Richard
  Leatherhead, 82
Sussex, Bignor, 80
  Bosham, 38-9
  Chichester, 47, 82
  Midhurst, 36
  Petworth House archives, 83–4
  Slinfold, 82
Swell, Lower, 49, 51, 114

Talbot, Robert, 32
Tankerville family, 88
Tann, Dr. J., 86
Taylor, Canon Charles S., 27, 129, 194
  Rev. Isaac, 182
  John (Bristol Librarian), 25, 26, 122, 189
  John, sen., 122
  Thomas T., 129
Telford, Thomas, 117
Tetbury, 38–9, 141
Tewkesbury, 98
  Abbey church, 80, 98
  Abbot of, 143
Tewkesbury Register & Magazine, 98, 175
Thames, source of, 141
Theyer, Anne, 43
  Charles, 19, 43 4
  John, 19, 43–4, 150–1
  John, sen., 43
  Thomas, 43
Thompson, E.M., 191
Thornbury, 89
Thorp, J.D., 51
Three Choirs, History of, 77
Thurnam, Dr. John, 26
Tidenham, 24, 96
Tockington Roman villa, 27, 110
Topographers of Suffolk, 15
Topographical Description of Gloucestershire, 46
Tower of London, princes in the, 145
Trotman family, 130
Trye, C.B., 77
Tuffley, 49

Turner, George, 73
Tyson, William, 22, 24, 42, 94, 95n, 99–100, 124, 171, 173, 176, 191

Uley, 69n
  Stoutshill in, 67
  Wresden in, 130
Unitarians, 94, 112–3, 183

Van der Gucht, Michael, 49
Veal (Veel), Mr., documents *penes*, 89
'vellomaniac', the, 105
vestments, church, 143
Victoria County History, 86, 135
Virginia, U.S.A., Berkeley Plantation in, 36, 40
  Company, 36
  Gloucestershire colonists in, 36
  papers relating to, 39
  Hanover County in, 91

Walpole, Horace, 67, 77, 83
Wantner, Abel, 20, 45–6, 60, 152
  Abel sen., 45
  Margaret, 45
Warburton, William, Bishop of Gloucester, 47
Warwickshire, Birmingham, 68
  Callowden, 36, 39
  Coventry, 31
Wattes, Thomas, 143
West, James (P.R.S.), 58, 159
Wharton, Henry, 47
White, John, 124
Whitefield, George, 57
Whitfield, Christopher, 63n
Wilkins, Ann (aft. Bigland), 64
William George's Sons Ltd., Bristol, 123
Williams, Miss M.E., 70

Willis, Browne, 21, 49–51, 52n, 59–60
  'Richard', 52n
Wilson, D.C.C., 89
Wiltshire, Bradford-on-Avon, 94
  Castle Combe, 143
  Devizes, 124
  Lacock, 70
  Swindon, 65
Winchcombe Abbey cartulary, 25, 54, 55, 114–5
Winchester College, 47
Winterbourne, 94
Witcombe Roman villa, 26, 80
Withington Peculiar, 132
Witts, G.B., 26
Wood, Anthony (à), 19 and n, 43–4, 150–1
  James ('Jemmy'), 75
Woodchester Roman villa, 23, 26, 79–80
Worcester, bishop of, 143
Worcester Diocesan Architectural Society, 114
Worcestershire, 20, 57
  Broadway, 24, 197
  Evesham, 62
  Evesham, Vale of, 21, 57
  Middle Hill (in Broadway), 105
Worcestre, Elizabeth, 31
  William (alias Botoner), 18, 19, 31–3, 36, 83, 84n, 140–3
  William (de), sen., 31
Wyatt, James, 81n

Yale University Library:
  Lindsay Fleming Collection, 78, 80, 138
  Osborn Collection, 37, 90
Yate, 124